Supporting and Promoting Wellbeing in the Higher Education Sector

This book provides innovative, practical tools to help combat declining personal wellbeing in the higher education workplace.

Divided into two sections, the book looks at wellbeing from institutional and individual levels. It outlines a framework for how wellbeing in the higher education workplace can be evaluated and clearly sets out initiatives for what can be done to improve faculty wellbeing. The book also explores issues such as the once vocational nature of academia, the extent to which institutions can provide allied health care and examines initiatives that individual faculty members have introduced for themselves.

Representing new ideas, perspectives and a variety of approaches to supporting and promoting wellbeing in the higher education workplace, this book will be of interest to academic staff as well as professional development personnel in higher education.

Angela R. Dobele is a retired Associate Professor in the College of Business and Law, RMIT University, Australia.

Lisa Farrell is a Professor in the College of Business and Law, RMIT University, Australia.

Wellbeing and Self-care in Higher Education
Editor: **Narelle Lemon**

Writing Well and Being Well for Your PhD and Beyond
How to Cultivate a Strong and Sustainable Writing Practice for Life
Katherine Firth

Prioritising Wellbeing and Self-Care in Higher Education
How We Can Do Things Differently to Disrupt Silence
Edited by Narelle Lemon

Navigating Tensions and Transitions in Higher Education
Effective Skills for Maintaining Wellbeing and Self-care
Edited by Kay Hammond and Narelle Lemon

Exploring Time as a Resource for Wellness in Higher Education
Identity, Self-care and Wellbeing at Work
Edited by Sharon McDonough and Narelle Lemon

Passion and Purpose in the Humanities
Exploring the Worlds of Early Career Researchers
*Edited by Marcus Bussey, Camila Mozzini-Alister, Bingxin Wang
and Samantha Willcocks*

Sustaining Your Wellbeing in Higher Education
Values-based Self-Care for Work and Life
Jorden A. Cummings

**Supporting and Promoting Wellbeing in the Higher
Education Sector**
Practices in Action
Edited by Angela R. Dobele and Lisa Farrell

For more information about this series, please visit: www.routledge.com/Wellbeing-and-Self-care-in-Higher-Education/book-series/WSCHE

Supporting and Promoting Wellbeing in the Higher Education Sector

Practices in Action

Edited by Angela R. Dobele and Lisa Farrell

Routledge
Taylor & Francis Group

LONDON AND NEW YORK

Designed cover image: © Getty Images

First published 2025
by Routledge
4 Park Square, Milton Park, Abingdon, Oxon OX14 4RN

and by Routledge
605 Third Avenue, New York, NY 10158

*Routledge is an imprint of the Taylor & Francis Group, an informa
business*

© 2025 selection and editorial matter, Angela R. Dobele and
Lisa Farrell; individual chapters, the contributors

The right of Angela R. Dobele and Lisa Farrell to be identified as
the authors of the editorial material, and of the authors for their
individual chapters, has been asserted in accordance with sections
77 and 78 of the Copyright, Designs and Patents Act 1988.

British Library Cataloguing in Publication Data
A catalogue record for this book is available from the British Library

ISBN: 978-1-032-25740-2 (hbk)
ISBN: 978-1-032-25739-6 (pbk)
ISBN: 978-1-003-28477-2 (ebk)

DOI: 10.4324/9781003284772

Typeset in Times New Roman
by KnowledgeWorks Global Ltd.

Contents

List of Figures and Tables   *vii*
Editor Biographies   *viii*
List of Contributors   *ix*
Series Editor Note   *xii*

Introduction: Wellbeing Matters   1
ANGELA R. DOBELE AND LISA FARRELL

PART I
Introduction to Part I: Faculty Wellbeing at
Institutional and Leadership Levels   5
ANGELA R. DOBELE AND LISA FARRELL

1 **Academic Support**   7
   DREW MCHUGH AND MELANIE TRASK

2 **Positive Wellbeing Within Workspaces**   23
   ANGELA R. DOBELE AND LISA FARRELL

3 **Provision of Wellbeing Services**   42
   EKANT VEER, MONA SOLTANI, AND TRACEY ROBINSON

PART II
Introduction to Part II: Wellbeing at the Individual Level   59
ANGELA R. DOBELE AND LISA FARRELL

4 **Academic Identities and Wellbeing Practices**   61
   MEG ELKINS

5 Innovative Practices for Supporting and Promoting Academic
   Faculty Wellbeing in the Higher Education Sector – Abstract   75
   KATE HYNES

6 Individual Wellbeing Practices for a Post-Pandemic University   96
   JONATHAN BOYMAL, SAM STERLING, CRAIG WILLIAMSON, YING ZHOU,
   AND PATRICK LYNCH

   Conclusion: Lessons Learnt   112
   ANGELA R. DOBELE AND LISA FARRELL

   Series Appendix   115

Figures and Tables

Figures

1.1 Reflection Drawing – Leading and Coaching to Support
Individual Wellbeing as Complementary to Organisational Wellbeing 20
2.1 Reflection Drawing – A Supportive Workplace Nurtures and
Empowers Employee Wellbeing 36
3.1 Impact of Wellbeing Services On- and Off-Campus 48
3.2 Reflection Drawing – A Holistic Approach to Building a
Wellbeing Culture 54
4.1 Reflection Drawing – My Personal Identity and Career Narrative 72
5.1 Illusion Constraint Feedback 80
5.2 Positive Conscious Belief Feedback 80
5.3 Prioritising Thoughts and Feelings That Feel Satisfying 89
5.4 Reflection Drawing – My Emotional Lighthouse 93
6.1 Overwhelmed in Academia – the Mental Health Impacts of
Academic Isolation 97
6.2 Rethinking What You Do and How You Do It 108
C.1 Word Cloud From the Author's Reflection Statements. 113

Tables

1.1 Successful Wellbeing Leaders 12
2.1 The Pop-Up Wellbeing Kit Bag 28
2.2 Working Space Personalisation Ideas 34
3.1 Summary of Risks and Benefits of Different Wellbeing
Intervention Models 49
5.1 Core Self-Evaluation Exercise 79
5.2 Illusion Constraints Exercise 81
5.3 Practicing Work-Life Balance and Wellbeing Exercise 84
5.4 The Emotional Guidance Scale 86
5.5 Writing Exercise 87
6.1 Formal and Informal Actions to Support Wellbeing 106

Editor Biographies

Angela R. Dobele is a retired Associate Professor in the field of marketing. During her academic career she was recognised as a transformative leader, skilled researcher and engaging teacher. Angela approached research based on her long running commitment to supporting staff and students in their career goals, including career progression and promotion. Angela's work was recognised through awards including College of Business and Law Collaborations in Learning and Teaching (2022) and Australia and New Zealand Marketing Academy (ANZMAC) Distinguished Marketing Educator Award (2019). She is the longest-serving RMIT Women Researchers' Network Steering Committee Chair (2018-2020) and is a committed peer coach, mentor and sponsor.

Lisa Farrell is a passionate champion of equality and diversity in the workplace and Professor of Economics. She has 25 years of experience in academia across the UK, Ireland and Australia. She is a health economist with expertise in wellbeing and mental health. Her work has a strong economic psychology focus to allow for a deep understanding regarding the integration of wellbeing with decision making and economic outcomes. She has published in leading journals across, economics, psychology, statistics and medicine highlighting her ability to communicate her research to many different audiences. Her research can be found in the number one ranked economics journal, The American Economic Review as well as high impact journals such as Social Science and Medicine among other leading international journals and specialist field journals. She has also jointly edited Churchill, S. A., Farrell, L., & Appau, S. (Eds.). (2020). Measuring, Understanding and Improving Wellbeing Among Older People. Springer Nature.

List of Contributors

Jonathan Boymal is an Associate Professor of Economics and Academic Director, Quality and Learning and Teaching Futures at the College of Business and Law, RMIT University. He has 25 years of higher education leadership experience across Melbourne, Hong Kong, Singapore and Vietnam. Jonathan's research focuses on the future of higher education. He holds a PhD in Economics and a Bachelor of Economics (Hons) from Monash University.

Meg Elkins is a behavioural and applied economist with research interests in societal and cultural economics. Her work focuses on those on the fringes to support sustainable livelihoods. She is equally interested in applying behavioural insights to societal issues, particularly around behavioural messaging. She has worked on projects with City of Melbourne, the Busking Project and the UK Behavioural Insights Unit Canva8. Meg is a member of the Behavioural Business Lab and the Centre for International Development. She is a regular TV, radio and print commentator on behavioural issues and decision-making processes.

Kate Hynes is an international trade economist currently working at Dublin City University in Ireland. Her research focuses on foreign direct investment (FDI). This includes government policies that affect FDI such as taxes, infrastructure investments and intellectual property rights. Kate has lectured across different countries including Ireland, Hong Kong, China, Saudi Arabia, and North Korea. Her international experience has sparked interest in how beliefs across cultures and core self-evaluations impact people's patterns of thought, habits, and decision-making process.

Patrick Lynch is an innovative learning and teaching professional passionate about academic capacity building and enhancing the student experience. His areas of interest include academic integrity, learning technologies, and artificial intelligence. Patrick's commitment to fostering a supportive and enriching academic culture resonates through his work

Drew McHugh is a dynamic and pragmatic organisational development professional with a proven track record in business partnering, workforce development, values and cultural transformation, change management, performance development, strategic leadership development, executive coaching and transformational facilitation. Drew holds a highly successful leadership and consulting background working in and consulting to large corporate and public sector enterprises including Financial Services, Higher Education, ATO, State Ministries and Infrastructure Services: Specialising in leadership, practical ethics, cultural development, executive coaching and strategic planning. In a career spanning over 20 years in people and organisational cultural development, Drew quickly develops a deep and practical understanding of the challenges and opportunities of the client groups he works and coaches with. As a McKinsey trained, senior member of the ANZ's Breakout and Cultural Transformation team, Drew assisted over 3000 leaders in many countries to powerfully re-assess and re-create their approach to effective people and cultural leadership.

Tracey Robinson is the Wellbeing Lead for Staff at the University of Canterbury. She holds an MBA from the University of Canterbury Business School where her research explored staff perceptions of wellbeing initiatives on campus. Her passion is for developing a wellbeing culture on campuses and supporting staff with their own wellbeing journey in all spaces.

Mona Soltani is a Ph.D. candidate in marketing at the University of Canterbury. She takes a mixed-methods approach to understanding marketing strategies, customer behaviour, social media marketing, and crisis communication. Her Ph.D. focuses on crisis management and communication on social media. Her current research seeks to understand how influential social media users can use their networks and influence to affect an organisation's brand image when a company faces a scandal or negative reputational effect. Her thesis highlights how different organisations should design communication strategies in response to a crisis or scandal shared via social media.

Sam Sterling has over 15 years of leadership experience in university, educational pathway and research contexts. In her role as Director (STEM) she champions access and inclusivity in science education and is passionate about fostering a thriving community of learners and educators in the programs within her directorate. A seasoned academic leader, she is acutely aware of the importance of physical, emotional and social wellbeing as the foundation on which academic success (in both teaching and learning contexts) is made possible. A lifelong learner, Sam has qualifications from: The University of Melbourne, Monash University, QUT and Griffith University (to date).

Melanie Trask is an experienced Executive Coach, Strategic HR Consultant and Change Manager. She has led and managed her own HR, Consulting and Sales Units, Specialist ER functions and also operated as an integral part of various Executive Leadership teams. High-level coaching, facilitation and strategic consulting skills are coupled with an HR/ER/IR employment law background and over 20 years of experience across a diverse range of industries, including banking & finance, engineering & manufacturing, FMCG's corporate law firms, tertiary education and not for profits. Best Practice in Coaching & Leadership Development, Change Management and Pragmatic HR/ER/IR People Solutions feature significantly in Melanie's background and remain central to her work. Insightful, pragmatic and highly approachable, Melanie quickly gains trust even in difficult, testing situations. Coaching Lead and Principal Consulting roles have been Melanie's recent engagements and have involved design and implementation of various coaching skills programs for Leaders as well as 1:1 executive coaching assignments. This has also included coaching as a means to achieve change interventions for numerous, complex enterprises facing significant change and transition and often in a fix-it, turnaround capacity. Melanie has also operated as an Executive member of a number of Leadership Business Transformation Teams to achieve significant results in finite time frames. Notably, Melanie was Head of Strategic Consulting for ANZ's Breakout and Cultural Transformation program and Practice Lead for Westpac's Commercial Banking Unit Leader as Coach change program. Originally qualified in Behavioral Sciences, "My best work occurs with Leaders and Organisations who are in transition or flux. I build individual connection, resilience and strength, assisting leaders to address the ever-present strategic, people and cultural change issues that are a constant in any Leadership role today". Melanie also has a post-grad business degree and is a fully accredited coach and coach supervisor.

Ekant Veer is a Professor of Marketing at the University of Canterbury. He is a multi-award winning teacher and researcher who focuses on using marketing to understand consumer practices and support social and individual wellbeing. His research has been published in numerous international journals, such as the *Journal of Marketing Management*, the *European Journal of Marketing*, and the *Journal of Public Policy and Marketing*. His own experiences with mental illness and navigating support systems afforded to him have given him a privileged insight into this space and the need to support faculty wellness in all spaces.

Craig Williamson is a learning and teaching professional with experience in developing curricula and assessment for undergraduate and postgraduate medical education, design, property, construction and business disciplines. His key focus is on assessment and how assessment allows students to demonstrate achieving program outcomes. He is also currently studying for a Master of Education at the University of Melbourne, specialising in assessment and pedagogy, and Leadership and Management.

Ying Zhou is a Senior Learning and Teaching Specialist at RMIT University. As an innovative educator, researcher, and information specialist with over 15 years of experience in higher education across Australia and New Zealand, Ying integrates scholarly excellence with a commitment to innovation and transformation in learning, teaching and student experience. Ying holds a PhD in Economics from Monash University, and her areas of research encompass economic modelling, financial markets, and scholarship of teaching and learning (SoTL). Ying has published her research findings in scholarly journals of international standing.

Series Editor Note curiosity and courage in navigating academic wellbeing: A note from the series editor

As the editor of the book series, *Wellbeing and Self-care in Higher Education: Embracing Positive Solutions*, I am delighted to celebrate this book as a part of the series collection. It has been a labour of love, and an accompaniment to the editors, Angela R. Dobele and Lisa Farrell, and authors for a number of years now. A project that has seen the changes in life's ups and downs, twists and turns, and lessons and healing. This book is a contribution to the book series that focuses on being proactive, empowering, and revealing the stories of working in higher education in a way that is akin to listening to a close friend share their insights and deepest personal experiences. It is about sharing voices, hearing voices, and attentive listening. It is about empowerment and agency.

My vision for this book series was to interrupt the closed doors, hidden and evaded conversations about our wellbeing and self-care in higher education, and bring these to the forefront so that wellbeing and self-care are integrated into our everyday lives. I wanted to create a space where we are not shamed or made to feel guilty; rather, a space where we can learn with and from one another about the ways we navigate and nurture our wellbeing in the workplace.

Through this series, I aim to foster a sense of openness, understanding, and collective growth, where we can share our stories, listen to each other's experiences, and empower one another to prioritise our wellbeing and self-care in the demanding world of higher education. It is about breaking down barriers, fostering dialogue, and embracing a culture of support and compassion for ourselves and our colleagues.

In this book, *Innovative Practices for Supporting and Promoting Wellbeing in the Higher Education Sector*, the editors Angela and Lisa have compiled a diverse collection of perspectives on the critical issue of academic wellbeing. The book acknowledges the growing wellbeing crisis in the higher education sector, exacerbated by the challenges posed by the COVID-19 pandemic, and the need for immediate attention and action. Divided into two parts we are invited to explore exploration into faculty wellbeing from an institutional and leadership perspective, and wellbeing at the individual level. The chapters are authored by scholars, practitioners, and those with lived experiences in academia, offering a range of theories, thoughts and practices aimed at enhancing academic wellbeing.

What I love about this book is that each chapter is underpinned by courage and curiosity. Curiosity and openness are the guiding principles that underpin each of these authors' ethos, fuelling an unwavering drive for continuous learning and personal growth. These core values have been instrumental in shaping academic identity and approaches to work.

Cultivating a mindset of curiosity has allowed each of these editors and authors to remain ever-inquisitive, constantly seeking new perspectives and insights that challenge their existing knowledge and assumptions. This openness to diverse viewpoints has enabled the rich dialogues we find in this book. We are invited to broaden our horizons, gaining a deeper understanding of the complexities that shape our work world. As readers, we are invited to explore the multifaceted challenges and triumphs that shape the academic experience. Each chapter encourages us to question our assumptions, to seek out new insights, and to embrace the richness that emerges when we approach these stories with open hearts and minds.

By embracing curiosity and openness, we amplify the stories that matter – the stories that have the power to inspire, to provoke, and to catalyse positive change within the higher education landscape. It is through these narratives that we can forge meaningful connections, recognising our shared struggles and celebrating our collective resilience.

As you journey through this book, I invite you to approach each chapter with a spirit of curiosity and openness, allowing yourself to be transformed by the narratives that unfold. It is in these stories, shared with courage and vulnerability, that we can find the wisdom, strength, and inspiration to navigate our own paths toward wellbeing and self-care.

Professor Narelle Lemon
Series Editor, Wellbeing and Self-care in Higher Education: Embracing Positive Solutions
Vice-Chancellor Professoriate Research Fellow & Professor in Education
Lead, Wellbeing and Education Research Community (WE)
Edith Cowan University, Perth Australia

Introduction

Wellbeing Matters

Angela R. Dobele and Lisa Farrell

Introduction

Academic wellbeing is important in an increasingly volatile and competitive higher education workplace. In this book, we consider academic faculty wellbeing from both the individual and institutional perspectives. Academic wellbeing is an important topic. We are in the midst of a higher education wellbeing crisis. Basia Spalek from University World News on 16 January 2021, suggests that:

> "The psychological well-being of university staff ... has traditionally been a marginalised issue ... Nevertheless, as a result of the globalisation and commodification of higher education, academic staff have experienced their workloads substantially increasing at the expense of healthy feelings of joy, curiosity and compassion, often leaving academics feeling low, anxious and overwhelmed" (Spalek, 2021, Additional Pressures section).

Evidence suggests that COVID-19 negatively impacted wellbeing in higher education, especially given the rapid changes required to deliver courses and rethink research projects in a world facing a pandemic of unprecedented proportions. Academia is still in flux, and more flex is required as academics meet the challenges of working in hybrid modes and new expectations of their employers and students. The growing prevalence and severity of the higher education wellbeing crisis warrants immediate and full attention. Shuston and Matson suggest that *higher education should lead the wellbeing revolution* (Shushok & Matson, 2021), and we agree.

This book focuses on the intersection of wellbeing and individual/institutional practice. To achieve this, we reflect on practices at the individual and institutional levels and highlight innovative approaches. This resource provides examples of what individuals and institutions are doing regarding better support, resourcing, and empowerment. Sometimes this means academics are doing it for themselves. Other times, it means senior management has stepped up and provided meaningful innovations.

DOI: 10.4324/9781003284772-1

We intend this book as a platform for readers to develop knowledge, skills, and confidence to be innovative in this space within their institutions. These innovations could involve changing work practices or introducing different options in teams, departments, faculties, or institutions. The impact of the global pandemic has reset the lens of work practices and wellbeing within the academic workforce, opening an international audience for the types of discussions and considerations we offer in this book. While many of the examples have been implemented in Australia, they have been selected under the criteria suitable for replication outside the Australian context. Most issues that impact academic wellbeing are general across the sector and the world.

Part of understanding any topic is to shine a spotlight upon it, research it, think about it, and talk about it with others far and wide. Therefore, in selecting chapter contributors, we engaged with scholars, practitioners and those with lived experience of academia to provide a collection of theories, thoughts and practices which focus on the enhancement of academic wellbeing from a number of different perspectives. Each chapter is authored by different people chosen not just according to their scholarship in the field but due to their passion for wellbeing practices and initiatives. We allow the authors to speak with their unique voices from their unique vantage points. As a result, we draw evidence from lived experience, professional practice, popular literature, grey literature, and scholarly research. Such an approach allows for a truly diverse collection of perspectives from which readers can consider what might work in their context.

Our authors use their lived experience to discuss the aspect of academic wellbeing that they feel is most important to them. They provide details of the things that work and the things that do not work from their career journeys. Each chapter ends with a reflection on the process of writing the chapter and being able to deliver advice to others. Helping others through shared experiences can be a cathartic and healing process and many of the reflections highlight this outcome. Challenging authors to also illustrate these reflections allowed us to focus on what was the most important message to share with others and the reflective images alone tell an interesting story. The book contains two parts, each comprising three chapters. Part I considers faculty wellbeing at the institutional and leadership levels, and Part II considers faculty wellbeing at the individual level.

The book is relevant to (i) wellbeing scholars, (ii) practitioners of wellbeing in higher education institutions, (iii) academics across the globe, and (iv) to education policy makers. It is written to offer practice-based ideas such that any reader might be able to benefit from the ideas within regardless of where they fit within the higher education workforce. Moreover, many of the initiatives discussed are transferrable outside the higher education sector.

We hope that through engaging with this book, our readers find many practical ideas they can implement to enhance their wellbeing and/or those in their workplace. The key message is to read, discuss, adopt, adapt and apply the tools and be wellbeing champions.

References

Spalek, B. (2021). *The forgotten mental health crisis: Pressures on staff.* University World News. https://www.universityworldnews.com/post.php?story=20210111140929866

Shushok, F., & Matson, T. (2021). Why higher education should lead the wellbeing revolution. *Gallup: Education.* https://www.gallup.com/education/328961/why-higher-education-lead-wellbeing-revolution.aspx

Part I

Introduction to Part I

Faculty Wellbeing at Institutional and Leadership Levels

Angela R. Dobele and Lisa Farrell

Introduction

The first three chapters of this resource consider wellbeing at the institutional/ faculty and leadership levels. Contributing authors provide two different perspectives, as consultants to, but separate from, higher education institutions, and as leaders within higher education institutions.

In Chapter 1, Melanie Trask and Drew McHugh offer a practitioner-based approach to wellbeing strategies for academics in higher education and move the conversation beyond platitudes towards programmes to foster a wellbeing mindset through coaching leadership. These authors have high-level coaching and strategic human resource backgrounds.

Chapter 2, written by Angela R. Dobele and Lisa Farrell, provides a reflective approach to wellbeing initiatives based on their multiple leadership roles and considered through the lens of indoor environmental quality.

Chapter 3, written by Ekant Veer provides the final chapter in this section. His Chapter 3, written by Ekant Veer, Mona Soltani and Tracey Robinson, provides the final chapter in this section. This chapter is also based on multiple leadership roles, in particular those held by Ekant. This chapter is also informed by Ekant's research in both social marketing and health promotion, and transformative consumer research, and Tracey's research and practical insight in leading wellbeing work in a university setting. This chapter explores the difficulties in offering wellbeing services, whether on-campus, off-site or online, and the risks of implementing any of these without first developing a wellbeing culture.

The global COVID-19 pandemic has refocused the lens on the importance of wellbeing and wellbeing strategies, and both institutions and individuals are looking for better practice. All three chapters in this section offer practical steps for having wellbeing discussions, suggested initiatives and focus for further deliberations.

DOI: 10.4324/9781003284772-2

Chapter 1

Academic Support

Drew McHugh and Melanie Trask

Introduction

Human energy is finite. Within human endeavour and industry, there will always be many more ideas than actual physical capacity to implement all ideas effectively. Harnessing your energy and that of those with whom you work and lead remains central to effective management, leadership, and, unsurprisingly, human wellbeing. There is a danger, though, that an increased focus on harnessing energy can lead to burnout, which is detrimental to wellbeing. Energy needs to be harnessed such that individuals remain aligned and focused on critical outcomes, as opposed to simply taking on more and more… and more. Even a computer will malfunction if overloaded, and we are, most certainly, not machines. The relationship between energy and successful leadership is reflected in the quotation below taken from Rao (2015) who considers a raft of leadership principles important to leading an organisation.

> ""Your first and foremost job as a leader is to take charge of your own energy and then help to orchestrate the energy of those around you", said management guru, Peter F Drucker."
>
> (Rao, 2015, p. 34)

In this chapter, we consider the challenge of harnessing energy without harming wellbeing in the context of the academic workspace. We approach this issue from a base of knowledge that the leadership this workspace requires has, arguably, changed fundamentally and forever in the run-up to and following COVID-19. With next to no support or training related to such fundamental changes, the clear irony is that those in the academic sector who teach leadership and management are not themselves tutored or experienced in these skills. Taking on a senior role in academia within the higher education sector today involves a continuous set of evolving challenges that have high-level impacts on individuals and the overall wellbeing of academic staff.

In today's academy, it is not enough to simply teach and research. Quality, high-level, and internationally acclaimed research, which is always of vital importance, is now a prerequisite for employment and advancement. The relentless funding

DOI: 10.4324/9781003284772-3

competition for ongoing research dollars means colleagues have now also become competitors. Resourceful impact, influence, and engagement with external industry, relevant business sectors, and aligned external bodies are expected. Teaching and learning, perhaps the fundamental core functions of academia, are subject to ongoing, high-level scrutiny. For example, details of required standards can be found in the benchmarks set by the United Kingdom's Higher Education Academy fellowship programme (Higher Education Academy, 2023). Some of the new changes that thrust on academics include mentoring and developing junior academics, taking on the role of transformational senior leader, and guiding others through tumultuous change while continuing to deliver new and dynamically evolving revenue streams.

The result is a more intensive labour process with academics pressured to teach exceptionally, publish internationally acclaimed research articles, submit competitive grant applications, engage with developments in digital teaching and learning, and participate in broad global knowledge exchange (Callaghan, 2022). In this respect, academic roles, particularly as they progress to the more senior echelons within higher education, have become more akin to private-sector general management leadership roles. The private enterprise's "cut-throat, dog-eat-dog" competitive environment is also increasingly becoming a feature of academic life.

Finally, recent times have seen unprecedented financial pressure courtesy of a global pandemic and the loss of international student revenue, along with the need to rapidly convert face-to-face learning to online or blended learning and digitally enabled learning modules, as well as a shift towards operating largely from home in relative isolation. Cumulatively these factors have resulted in the transition to the "new normal" taking on Herculean proportions for academics and academic leaders.

Given this current landscape, the importance of working with and developing an organisational wellbeing programme has perhaps never been greater. In our professional roles, we have listened to, coached, supported, debriefed, mentored, and buddied academics for several decades and know firsthand that leadership roles today can be extremely difficult and lonely. They are the roles for which, in general, academics are often not trained or appropriately supported. Here, we share our insights into how to successfully lead while maintaining a healthy wellbeing status in the modern academy.

Wellbeing in the Workplace

The best way to start our discussion is by asking: where does wellbeing in higher education begin? We maintain it starts with leaders and leadership principles more broadly, and also with the shared accountability of an organisation's people. Arguably, all individuals in an organisational setting are, at any time and context, leaders for the cultivation of a wellbeing mindset.

Organisations have the responsibility to develop a positive workplace that values wellbeing as a legitimate concern, much as it does for physical health and safety. Working to reduce the stigma associated with wellbeing issues, providing avenues to build positive emotional states and psychological margin or capital

(Luthans et al., 2007) via a focus on individual signature strengths and working to emphasise ongoing resilience (Seligman, 2006). Further, while performance and development reviews may "strengthen bureaucracy" (Cope, 1997, p. 461), they are also a key strategy for building motivated staff (Argyris, 1991; Posthuma & Campion, 2008) and "allow managers and employees to communicate, provide feedback, and share ideas, information and opinions" (Alexander, 2006, p. 9).

However, an inherent critical issue is the tension between organisational and individual responsibilities for wellbeing (Phung et al., 2022). As experienced coaches across multiple organisations, we have noted a similarity in many wellbeing approaches offered to staff and leaders who are charged with implementing such approaches. First, organisations provide a platform for encouragement, reinforcement, and a means to achieve wellbeing. Second, individual employees are charged with incorporating wellbeing strategies into their work lives as they would for physical care (through daily routines for sleep, diet, and exercise).

Between the organisation and individual staff are the leaders who have distinct accountability to role model wellbeing as a fundamentally legitimate and worthwhile pursuit. The role of wellbeing champion or role model could be formally or informally offered and might also include some form of recognition. The ultimate payoff is that the overall wellbeing of an organisation's people works simultaneously in successfully meeting organisational goals. The clear identification of responsibility in this way allows for a structured approach to consider roles and responsibilities for nurturing wellbeing across an organisation.

Moving Wellbeing Forward

Having identified the traditional framework and accountability considerations, this section considers how higher education leaders can actively promote and support wellbeing. In our experience, there are several flaws in the traditional model. What is required within academic leadership is careful consideration of organisational strategies that best support individual academics in their work and wellbeing.

First, any wellbeing approach must be jointly entwined across *work* and *wellbeing*, not mutually exclusive or ignoring the latter completely. A joint approach recognises both the formal and informal leadership within disciplines and departments and their impacts across key stakeholder groups. Second, the focus needs to move beyond the traditional model of employee assistance programmes (EAPs), where the trap could be to assume services have been offered and thus, no more can or should be offered, or to leave responsibility for wellbeing with staff and assume no further engagement in wellbeing practices or promotions is required.

While the services offered by EAPs can be highly effective, and indeed lifesaving in a crisis, the biggest single stumbling block we've seen is employee reluctance to use them. Barriers include stigma perceptions and lack of trust (Matthews et al., 2021; Milot, 2019). EAPs tend to be only utilised at times of crisis (Csiernik, 2011). However, we are trying to avoid reaching such situations, so need to consider prior support.

Typically, most of an organisation's wellbeing investment budget is allocated to EAP services, which most staff never utilise. Such a discrepancy between provision and utilisation implies most staff will not benefit from this investment. Additionally, these employees do not have access to preventative wellbeing support; thus, too often an employee's mental health is already at risk by the time they seek specialist EAP input.

In developing a more proactive approach to wellbeing, thoughtful and advanced options centre around techniques such as Appreciative Inquiry or Open Systems Communication Forums. These approaches engage key employee stakeholders and seek their input into what makes effective wellbeing programmes. Seeking input on a range of wellbeing perspectives recognises that one size does not fit all. Actively canvassing input into what effectively supports wellbeing across several different perspectives and thoughtfully considering where a wellbeing budget would be best utilised provides a multifaceted and diverse wellbeing framework that could be better positioned to meet the needs of the entire workforce.

Previous research has described such an approach as the co-designed workplace wellbeing strategy (Hurria, 2023), which firmly moves the focus and practice away from something done *to* employees to something done *with* them. Further, there is the added benefit of identifying and supporting wellbeing champions to operate across your workplace. The idea of wellbeing champions is discussed in detail by The Wellbeing Lab's co-founder, Dr Michelle McQuaid, and is as discussed in detail in Campbell (2023).

Co-designing Workplace Wellbeing

Quality conversations and employee input are essential in developing the organisational approach to wellbeing and are also essential in developing and supporting individual wellbeing mindsets, as well as cultivating a collective norm that values and prioritises wellbeing first and foremost. From our experiences within various industries, organisations, and cultures, spanning decades, this is the vital duopoly we see in every organisation that has managed to successfully establish wellbeing-focused workplaces.

A meaningful connection to a shared purpose, combined with strategies that develop resilience by building on an individual's inherent strengths and enhancing their overall psychological capital, are the best features of what we would consider innovative organisational wellbeing solutions (Luthans et al., 2007). Such innovative organisational wellbeing solutions also need to include regular one-on-ones, and regular and structured progress development review discussions with direct managers on work matters (not just yearly at performance review time). The capacity, trust, and confidence to reach out and discuss pertinent issues before they become insurmountable are also important factors.

While these systems of review, development, and open discussions are not new, the consistent, conscientious application of them as a means to further wellbeing is new in this context of higher education. Formal and informal mentoring and buddy programmes, wellbeing champions and, more recently, higher-level appointments of work-based psychologists into Chief Wellbeing Officer roles (Trinca, 2022a and 2022b), continue to address and cater for workplace wellbeing. Each strategy is formulated on actively canvassing input and communicating what an organisation's people could and would find valuable from a wellbeing perspective.

These factors (quality conversations and employee input) are pertinent when considering managing change agendas and in times of outside pressure or stress (such as our recent COVID-19 experiences), particularly when such agendas invariably involve loss of certainty, control, and loss of status. In particular, in the higher education industry, the wellbeing of academics has come under increased scrutiny (Wray & Kinman, 2022), and rightly so. In particular, previous research has highlighted psychosocial hazards that are specific to academia, including those inherent within academic employment roles, along with key workplace challenges (Strevens et al., 2023; Wray & Kinman, 2022). Overall, the most frequently experienced wellbeing hazard continues to be poorly executed change management (McQuaid, 2023). What is most commonly missing is face-to-face, direct communication from managers to employees around the change agenda and the impact on roles such changes will have (de Jager, 1994; Larkin & Larkin, 1994; Richardson & Denton, 1996). In our experience, the way to protect wellbeing in a change environment is through open, quality conversations with employee input and consultation on the proposed change agenda.

Invest in Coaching Conversations and Leadership Development

Quality conversations and coaching conversations, in particular, draw on the competencies of advanced listening skills, powerful questioning ability, and reflective practices, offering individual, holistic personal development, which, because it is internally self-driven, tends to last over time. Such self-motivation, important in any workplace, may be particularly well suited to academics who value autonomy and agency (Callaghan, 2022).

Similarly, maintaining a degree of autonomy or input into how work is tackled, "having a say", and the capacity to experience a degree of success or, ultimately, mastery in your given area, as well as a strong sense of progress and ownership of outcomes and results, all foster a sense of purpose, motivation, intrinsic connection, and resultant mental wellbeing (Pink, 2011). Coaching conversations inherently build on all these attributes.

As far back as the industrial revolution and Marx and Engels' (1967) Communist Manifesto, the alienation of workers from their labour and output had deleterious impacts on wellbeing. It makes sense that the opposite may well have a positive impact. In practice, we have found that indeed it does – at least from our decades of experience! A workplace that communicates, coaches, develops, and fosters a collective wellbeing mindset in individual employees may well be the silver bullet that many organisations have been searching for. We have witnessed that such institutions generally have employees who are more successful at achieving organisational goals.

Perhaps of most significance are senior leaders who regularly articulate and act according to wellbeing principles to foster wellbeing in themselves, their workplaces, and individuals, as the organisational norm (Trinca, 2022a and 2022b). Given our professional roles are frequently connected to coaching leaders, we have included a list of the characteristics of leaders and leadership we have witnessed as effective in enhancing wellbeing and so encourage the leaders we interact with to reflect on. The focus here is not on merely achieving organisational goals but on achieving organisational goals *while being mindful of employee wellbeing*. We have compiled our suggestions for successful wellbeing leaders in Table 1.1.

Table 1.1 Successful Wellbeing Leaders

- Have a primary focus is to lead, nurture, and develop others.
- Act beyond the busy day-to-day transactional goals that might come at the expense of employee wellbeing.
- Work primarily *on* the business, in terms of developing strategy, direction, and overall vision, not *in* the business, from a purely operational or "doing" lens.
- Remove roadblocks. They do not instigate or build roadblocks (either consciously or unconsciously) and remain watchful of unintended consequences of their micro and macro policy-setting.
- Develop strong interdependent teams with clear, purposeful goals and regularly and consistently celebrate milestones and achievements.
- Bear pain, and do not inflict pain.
- Can say "No" and hold to it. They stay focused on key priorities, knowing intrinsically that they simply cannot do *everything* on the "to do list".
- Understand that all their actions as leaders send a message – including the myriad of emails, texts, phone calls, and messages – send a message.
- Understand the wellbeing implications of communications sent at all times of the night or day, over weekends, public holidays, and regardless of or during periods of annual leave.
- Send messages that reinforce mental wellbeing as the required norm, including leading by example (such as leaving work early some nights to attend a child's concert, a partner's special birthday, or taking time out).
- Know the intrinsic needs of being human, understanding that we all crave connections, meaningful pursuits, and need reflective thinking, time, and space above the incessant din of life. They are aware that allowing for these needs enhances an employee's ability to make creative connections and find innovative solutions.
- Understand that we are not machines and that even a machine will cease to function if consistently overloaded.
- Prioritise quality time with their people, regularly, both on a structured and unstructured basis.

Coaching Leaders

In this section, we draw from our joint professional experience to present a series of examples of wellbeing-focussed leadership through coaching as this is our joint area of expertise. While the examples are based on experience, the details of the individuals and companies are obviously not noted to preserve confidentiality and the cases are presented in a hypothetical framework.

Let's begin by exploring the role of coaching leaders and employees within organisations. Coaching[1] is most often utilised to assist a competent and satisfactory employee to move beyond their current performance level, transition to a new role or, deal with factors that somehow are inhibiting their effectiveness. In our experience, wellbeing, or lack of it, is often a key component to facilitate these transitions. The gift of reflective time, the space to think and ruminate on the hypothetical, to work on the business if only for a brief time rather than being consumed by the day-to-day operations in the business, is routinely highlighted by our coaches as one of the benefits of coaching. Additionally, coaching follows the coachee's agenda, situating them as the expert in their own work and life dilemmas, and reinforces their own solutions to their problems, as well as their own successes and mastery in implementing these solutions. Significantly, time for personal reflection and thinking, a place to *be* rather than to manically *do*, remains a key cornerstone to wellbeing.

Coaching conversations can be powerful and effective when they are helping an employee to challenge a strongly held belief that they are undeserving of time away from work and debunking the increasingly witnessed toxic positivity myth (Bosveld, 2021). Similarly, a skilful coach can work with an individual to foster their understanding of both their formal and informal spheres of control, and how to control the things that are controllable and accept the rest. Importantly, accepting what we cannot change does not mean condoning or turning a blind eye to bad news or behaviours, but it does mean actively choosing to focus our energies on the things we actually do have power over (Unmind, 2022b).

Additionally, coaching is reported by coachees to be a highly effective means to increase self-awareness, self-confidence, specifically in decreasing self-limiting thoughts and beliefs, and effective self-management and leadership of themselves (Sinclair, 2021). Unconscious expectations are highlighted, and for many participants, unrealistic expectations are often uncovered, along with the ability to lead themselves and others with more compassion and self-acceptance. Building proficiency, listening, questioning, influencing, and persuading skills, as well as the capacity to recognise multiple perspectives and develop high-level empathy for others, are also regularly cited as benefits to coaching.

Overall leadership style, relationships with others, with power and with conflict, and the opportunity to reflect on these issues in a mindful way enable the coachee to be more thoughtful, efficient, and effective going forward with their approach to tasks, to others, and to achieve organisational goals. Finally, the coaching space also offers the chance to explore and reflect on work-life balance and other responsibilities, particularly regarding family. Coaching supports individuals in making links within work to parts of their life outside of work, adding a helpful holistic viewpoint. Coaching in this way helps explore and find insights around how things in our lives interconnect (Sime & Jacob, 2018).

At the conclusion of our coaching engagements – anywhere up to six months and sometimes for far longer – we routinely seek feedback as to what the coachee has found most valuable. The one consistent piece of feedback we receive about coaching's effectiveness as an intervention is the reflective space it enables (Cushion, 2018). Space, time, support, and collegiate partnership provide the capacity to reflect deeply on surprises, failures, and frustrations, as well as successes. At the root of all this lie personal goals, values, ambitions, and efforts, which are at once cognitive, emotional, and behavioural. This reflects the juncture of head, heart, and hands, which are constantly in motion and as with any physical anatomy in need of rest, rejuvenation, and re-energising to remain strong and effective. It seems a space for mindful reflection may well become an ongoing means or prerequisite for consistent and sustainable wellbeing in our leaders and in people more generally.

Example 1: Change as a Wellbeing Pathway

This example is based on a CEO in an organisation that faced an uncertain future if it was unable to make some aggressive changes. The CEO felt frustrated at the lack of buy-in to his vision, which he considered one that would save the company and secure its future as a major employer within the region. His comments highlight this frustration:

> *Why can't they see this?*
> *This is not a luxury; this is do or die*
> *My change agenda is the only viable way forward for us all*

In coaching sessions, we agreed with his summation totally and carefully allowed him to discover that this was in fact "his" change agenda and not that of the others in the company. The question then became how to engage others in his agenda, such that it became their own. To achieve this, the change agenda had to be seen as essential for their own employability, security and wellbeing going forward as well as for the company leaders.

As a result of this insight, the CEO set up simple, informal communication sessions where he regularly invited diverse groups of employees from across the organisation to share breakfast with him, on company time as part of their shift. Attendance was optional, but the opportunity was extended to all, and the sessions, over time, became much coveted. At the sessions, employees worked through the implications of the change agenda with a free and open exchange and questions allowed by all. Importantly, these were not one-off events or even a series of events, but a regular item in the CEO's diary and one that he learned to value immensely and continued to run weekly over his eight-year tenure. He reported back that it enabled him to tap into any concerns or developing issues at the outset and provide frank and honest conversations, as well as brainstorming and workable solutions offered and owned by those affected. Simultaneously, an employee change programme was implemented across the organisation giving individual employees an opportunity to both quantify their existing work environment as well as define what they would like it to be. This knowledge then informed a large-scale work improvement programme, involving dedicated work groups, and incorporating changes that were devised, implemented, and owned by the team. Importantly, physiological safety improved, and the wellbeing of the workforce became synonymous with achievement, pride in meeting work goals, and overcoming hitherto too-difficult-to-tackle obstacles, while providing an ongoing viable future for the organisation that all had contributed to.

Example 2: Wellbeing Staff Development

In a different organisational setting, by coaching across a team of senior leaders, we focused on co-created solutions. In this example, a group of senior leaders in a large multinational organisation became empowered to conduct regular one-on-one, quality development discussions with their individual team members. Emphasis was on goal clarity and achievement of key performance indicators (KPIs), as well as providing one-on-one assistance, development in customer engagements, and ultimately securing the sales goals of the organisation. Over time, these leaders became self-nominated "Development Heads" and their centres boasted superior results with highly engaged employees, dedicated to learning from "the maestro" and developing their skills as highly employable resources. As a result, poor performance declined, as did overall sick leave rates. Moreover, the corresponding employee wellbeing and engagement scores were some of the highest on record within the company. Once again, this speaks to the power of allowing employees to be part of the conversations that define the way work is done to achieve success. Connections build trust and are rewarded with dedicated employees.

Example 3: Wellbeing in Times of Difficulty

It is an important distinction that effective leaders do not ignore poor performance or become fearful of challenging their people in the context of appropriate development. Rather, wellbeing leaders are actively involved in assisting in navigating the highs and lows we all experience in our work lives. There is an implicit understanding that wellbeing ranges from languishing (low levels of wellbeing) to thriving (high levels of wellbeing) (Keys, 2002, as described in Mishra, 2017). Wellbeing as a range or continuum can become a particularly challenging proposition for a leader. Understanding the key purposes, principles, and codes to which one agrees and believes in leading are incredibly important. These provide the handrails for supporting the waxing and waning of a wellbeing curve for themselves and their people. Also important is applying the balancing ingredient of compassion and regard for what it is to be human.

In this context, this example involves the case of a senior academic leader who displayed the effective application of this mix of skills when he was faced with a situation that involved several material breaches of ethical standards. The leader courageously assessed the impact of these breaches through not just a professional, policy or code set of lenses, but also the lens of the wellbeing of all stakeholders. The ultimate result was not just holding those responsible to account, but also considering how all stakeholders would best be supported in navigating their wellbeing over the short, mid, and longer terms with this challenge to their ethical framework. Clearly articulated support mechanisms and active application of these, through transparent communication, counselling, coaching, special leave, and open-door conversations, greatly assisted the weathering of the inherent wellbeing fluctuations during and after the time of immediate crisis.

"The goal is not to constantly 'improve' our levels of wellbeing, rather it is to become more impactful and active participants in caring for our wellbeing, so that we can effectively engage and function well at work as we navigate the highs and lows, we all experience" (The Wellbeing Lab, 2021, p. 5). The leader's role in this context is to actively observe and support that navigation.

Example 4: Coaching as a Wellbeing Intervention

Working with a newly appointed academic leader tasked with holding a highly talented research team together and avoiding costly attrition, as coaches, we were struck by the leader's high level of personal commitment. The leader's deeply conscientious type A personality demonstrated an all-consuming passion to hold this team together, not only to prevent the loss of valuable skills but also to "save them" and enable their efforts to be recognised again within the organisation.

There were a host of other factors affecting the team dynamic here that this leader had no control over, including an Academic Dean, appointed just three months after the leader's arrival, with a cost-cutting agenda and who made it abundantly clear that he no longer supported the research work of this team. The task, over time, became the winding down and retrenching of the entire team, wearing the fallout in a highly personal manner – all of which nearly broke this leader. At the height of the leader's distress, they were referred to a coach, and discovered which responsibilities were theirs, and which belonged to someone else. This leader also experienced their own personal awakening to a tendency to embody a "Mother Theresa" rescue persona. Without this one-on-one, pertinent, confidential, and highly effective coaching intervention, this leader's wellbeing would have been in severe jeopardy. Importantly, what was advocated here was not an abdication of the leader's role but recognising where their energy was best spent. In this regard, the leader focused on highly effective outplacement support for their team, ensuring their inherent skill sets were utilised effectively – albeit elsewhere.

Example 5: Coaching to Practice What You Preach

In this example, we recall coaching a busy senior academic in a challenging leadership role. She was a mother of three primary school-aged children, with a home renovation underway, multiple active memberships in school and childcare centre committees, and a husband who travelled for work three weeks every month. What surprised us

was how long it took for the wheels to fall off and, when they inevitably did, how ap-
palled this leader was by our suggestion to find some time for herself, starting with just
half an hour a day to regenerate.

Impossible! How self-indulgent! I do not have time!
Our response to her was
*Think of all that you give to others every moment of every day. Do you re-
ally value yourself so little? We are suggesting half an hour a day to replenish
yourself.*

Accepting that challenge, though begrudgingly at first, this executive worked into
her daily routine, a small window of time, just for herself. Those times provided space
for reflection, and solutions were born. She has also understood that "self-care is more
than tub soaks or country walks. It's also about setting workplace boundaries, knowing you simply cannot do it all, switching off, saying no, and knowing what's vital
to prioritise" (Unmind, 2022b, p. 13). All this was achieved through ongoing quality
conversations with her direct manager, peers, and direct reports.

As coaches, we have had experiences where we know we have bought people back
from the brink of a wellbeing abyss. Thankfully, these remain extreme and rare cases
but are a warning to us of the need to protect our wellbeing in all arenas of our lives.

Future Wellbeing Support

Wellbeing is a relatively recent addendum to the health and safety agenda (Trinca,
2023), finding its unique niche initially in work related to stress claims or psychological injuries of the 90s. The addition coincided with the Great Wall Street
Crash, followed later by the Global Financial Crisis of 2008. More recently, we
have experienced the confusion and challenge of the COVID-19 pandemic. Such
global shocks resulted in whole-scale restructuring, reshaping, and mass redundan-
cies globally in an effort by employers to manage escalating organisational costs.
In most instances, these come at a high cost to employee wellbeing.

Physical health and wellbeing are now effectively synonymous, recognised
as equally fundamental to all workplace wellness initiatives, and perhaps even
more so now with the recent global wave of anxiety and depression triggered
by increasing levels of physical and social isolation problems resulting from the
COVID-19 pandemic. The advent of the pandemic and the necessity to work
remotely and essentially isolated at home also further blurred the traditional
boundaries of work and personal lives. Physical, mental, and work-life wellbeing
have become irretrievably intertwined in hybrid roles that encompass both the
personal and professional from beyond the confines of the traditional office
setting (Unmind, 2022a).

Perhaps as a direct result, we have seen a plethora of employee wellbeing
programmes and events being adopted by companies in more recent times – from
"R U OK" days (described in detail in Mok et al., 2016), to allowing staff to bring
children, partners, and pets to work and altruistic company sponsored Volun-
teer Leave to engender feel-good support and teamwork for a nominated charity

(Baird et al., 2022). These efforts are part of organisations' legitimate desires to address and, perhaps more important from a liability perspective, be seen to proactively and robustly address, the topic of holistic wellbeing.

Although noble in their efforts to raise awareness of wellbeing, and certainly aimed at reducing associated stigmas, such programmatic or event-based wellbeing initiatives remain at times little better than glib lip service or tick-the-box attempts to placate Top Management, HR, People and Culture departments, or Occupational Health and Safety Committees. Against this backdrop, one example from our collective experience of where organisations get this consistently wrong stands out: programmatic wellbeing tokenism. This not only doesn't work but can be counterproductive for wellbeing.

The following example comes from, ironically, a health company we worked with, who espoused holistic wellbeing from an external marketing platform and an internal values perspective, regularly offering a variety of internal wellbeing programmatic events for staff. Daily meditation sessions were offered, complete with attendant expert meditator, prayer bells, and a purpose-made meditation room, as well as a company gym and pool. Company-funded lunches were served each week, boasting healthy and nutritious fare and with the most current wellbeing gurus attending as guest speakers.

Despite more junior employees and middle managers enjoying these events immensely, Senior Managers and Executives remained largely absent. They were some of the most stressed and unwell individuals we have ever worked with. Long work hours, arduous travel schedules, meetings held as early as 6 am and as late as midnight and over weekends or public holidays, and individual annual leave balances well in excess of 80 days were commonplace.

The inevitable advent of burnout, punctuated with intermittent periods of total physical exhaustion and illness, were worn as badges of honour and recognised as the dividing range between lower management and the "truly motivated" higher organisational leaders. The wellbeing mindset embraced so publicly, complete with many external accolades and industry awards, did not apply to more senior employees, and in fact was relegated to those considered less dedicated or with limited ambition and drive, who were certainly not regarded as long-term future leaders of the company. An all-pervasive mantra of "I'll sleep when I'm dead" was actively perpetuated by the organisation's founding entrepreneur and heavily subscribed to by all direct reports, despite operating within the health and wellness sector! This is a perfect example of not walking the walk.

Wellbeing is the business of all employees regardless of seniority. Toxic senior leader cultures impact the wellbeing of those charged with the most responsibility and leave an organisation vulnerable to burnt out, ineffective leadership. This example clearly illustrates that programmatic wellbeing "tokenism" does not work and can in fact be counterproductive.

There is a broader organisational imperative in any wellbeing initiative. Despite the existence of world-class programmes and events, organisations who fail to take into account the context and impact of their workplace's socially constructed environment risk, at best, their wellbeing initiatives serving as mere platitudes and, at worst, fostering deep-seated cynicism and resentment of wellbeing initiatives in their employees.

Conclusion

Decades of professional experience coaching within organisation across a number of sectors and a more recent focus on the higher education sector has taught us some interesting truths about the effective practice of wellbeing leadership with the workplace. In this chapter, we have shared some of these learnings in the hope that they will be valuable to others and assist in the drive towards wellbeing-focused leadership.

To summarise, we believe that to be successful in protecting your own wellbeing it is essential to make it personal and first develop your own wellbeing mindset. In other words, developing a wellbeing mindset for you and your organisation starts with how you as an individual embody it. Or not. Much like the ownership of their own physical wellbeing, employees must also take active responsibility for nurturing their own health and wellbeing with the support, means, and encouragement of their organisations.

The key lesson from this chapter is to reflect on how to legitimise wellbeing as a worthy pursuit for yourself and others. What messages does an organisation send when upholding certain stereotypes or role models? With this question in mind, both formal and informal leaders in organisations can foster wellbeing as a legitimate workplace concern. We recommend that leaders keep in mind:

- The behaviours that they recognise and reward.
- The employees they promote.
- The messages they personally send via their own actions and behaviours including the things they do not do.
- How they make work meaningful for their people, engaging them in shared hopes and effort to achieve results.
- The day-to-day working environment that they build through all of the above.

Organisations should focus on their messaging by considering the following:

- Building workplace wellbeing strategy around open conversations and employee input from a multi-dimensional wellbeing framework.
- The unintended consequences within the workplace wellbeing strategy that could otherwise normalise moments of difficulty and challenge.
- Showcasing institutional and individual achievements that can positively impact wellbeing.
- Clearly articulating what organisational workplace wellbeing strategy effectiveness looks like.
- Reviewing wellbeing strategies and initiatives through a systems lens to ensure organisational activities take a holistic approach to wellbeing.

In this chapter, we have explored the wellbeing strategies we've seen in the course of our practitioner careers. We further considered wellbeing strategies that could be implemented for successful wellbeing leadership and offer suggestions for leaders and institutions in higher education. We conclude by posing a final question to our readers,

What can you do today to support your workplace wellbeing strategy?

Reflections from Chapter Authors

Our intention, in much of our work in the organisational wellbeing space, has been to seek to move the conversation beyond the platitudes of "R U OK?" days. We've sought to incorporate our experiences in coaching during times of unprecedented change. Fostering a wellbeing mindset in individuals remains central for academic welfare and is consistent with effectively achieving broader organisational goals. However, for wellbeing to be central, there must be clear and firm links between individual, organisation, academia, and professional goals (as depicted in our reflection drawing, Figure 1.1). In such an approach, supporting individual staff must be complementary to overall organisational wellbeing. We offer this final question as food for thought: with these lessons and learnings shared, what can you do today to support your workplace wellbeing strategy?

Figure 1.1 Reflection Drawing – Leading and Coaching to Support Individual Wellbeing as Complementary to Organisational Wellbeing

Notes

1 Here we distinguish coaching as being different but complementary to mentoring. Mentoring typically is about imparting the wisdom of experience, while coaching typically occurs through observation and effective questioning techniques, allowing the counterpart to challenge their own ways of thinking and create a path forward that is owned by them exclusively.

References

Alexander, D. M. (2006). *How do 360 degree performance reviews affect employee attitudes, effectiveness and performance?* (Seminar Research Paper Series, Paper 8). https://digitalcommons.uri.edu/lrc_paper_series/8

Argyris, C. (1991). Teaching smart people how to learn. *Harvard Business Review, 69*(3), 4–15.

Baird, M., Hamilton, M., Dinale, D., Gulesserian, L., & Heron, A. (2022). Broadening our conception of Leave: Leave to care for self or others over the life course. In I. Dobrotić, S. Blum, & A. Koslowski (Eds.), *Research handbook on leave policy* (pp. 368–383). Edward Elgar Publishing.

Bosveld, E. (2021). *Positive vibes only.* https://sandberg.nl/media/document/original/positivevibesonly_evabosveld.pdf

Callaghan, G. (2022). Introducing a coaching culture within an academic faculty. *International Journal of Evidence Based Coaching and Mentoring, 20*(1), 83–92.

Campbell, J. (2023). *Why "wellbeing champions" are a great addition to the workplace.* https://www.hrleader.com.au/wellbeing/23680-why-wellbeing-champions-are-a-great-addition-to-the-workplace

Cope, G. H. (1997). Bureaucratic reform and issues of political responsiveness. *Journal of Public Administration Research and Theory, 7*(3), 461–471.

Csiernik, R. (2011). The glass is filling: An examination of employee assistance program evaluations in the first decade of the new millennium. *Journal of Workplace Behavioral Health, 26*(4), 334–355.

Cushion, C. J. (2018). Reflection and reflective practice discourses in coaching: A critical analysis. *Sport, Education and Society, 23*(1), 82–94.

de Jager, P. (1994). Communicating in times of change. *Journal of Systems Management, 45*(6), 28.

Higher Education Academy. (2023). *Professional standards framework for teaching and supporting learning in higher education.* AdvanceHE. https://s3.eu-west-2.amazonaws.com/assets.creode.advancehe-document-manager/documents/advance-he/PSF%202023%20-%20Screen%20Reader%20Compatible%20-%20final_1675089549.pdf

Hurria, J. (2023). Burnout – an exponential rise. *Journal of Organizational Psychology, 23*(1), 37–46.

Larkin, T. J., & Larkin, S. (1994). *Communicating change: Winning employee support for new business goals.* McGraw Hill Professional.

Luthans, F., Avolio, B. J., Avey, J. B., & Norman, S. M. (2007). Positive psychological capital: Measurement and relationship with performance and satisfaction. *Personnel Psychology, 60*(3), 541–572.

Marx, K., & Engels, F. (1967). *The communist manifesto. 1848* (S. Moore, Trans.). Penguin.

Matthews, L. R., Gerald, J., & Jessup, G. M. (2021). Exploring men's use of mental health support offered by an Australian employee assistance program (EAP): Perspectives from a focus-group study with males working in blue-and white-collar industries. *International Journal of Mental Health Systems, 15*(1), 1–17.

McQuaid, M. (2023). *Can you spot the psychosocial hazards in your team?* https://www.michellemcquaid.com/can-you-spot-the-psychosocial-hazards-in-your-team/

Milot, M. (2019). *Stigma as a barrier to the use of Employee Assistance Programs. A Work-reach Solutions research report.* http://hdl.handle.net/10713/8515

Mishra, M. (2017). Understanding well-being: A practical approach. *Indian Journal of Health & Wellbeing, 8*(10), 1133–1135.

Mok, K., Donovan, R., Hocking, B., Maher, B., Lewis, R., & Pirkis, J. (2016). Stimulating community action for suicide prevention: Findings on the effectiveness of the Australian R U OK? Campaign. *International Journal of Mental Health Promotion, 18*(4), 213–221.

Phung, V.-H., Sanderson, K., Pritchard, G., Bell, F., Hird, K., Wankhade, P., Asghar, Z., & Siriwardena, N. (2022). The experiences and perceptions of wellbeing provision among English ambulance services staff: A multi-method qualitative study. *BMC Health Services Research, 22*(1), 1–14.

Pink, D. H. (2011). *Drive: The surprising truth about what motivates us.* Penguin.

Posthuma, R. A., & Campion, M. A. (2008). Twenty best practices for just employee performance reviews: Employers can use a model to achieve performance reviews that increase employee satisfaction, reduce the likelihood of litigation and boost motivation. *Compensation and Benefits Review, 40*(1), 47–55.

Rao, M. S. (2015). Twenty-one success sutras for chief executives: How to lead during turbulent times. *Human Resource Management International Digest, 23*(2), 34–37.

Richardson, P., & Denton, D. K. (1996). Communicating change. *Human Resource Management, 35*(2), 203–216.

Seligman, M. E. (2006). *Learned optimism: How to change your mind and your life.* Vintage.

Sime, C., & Jacob, Y. (2018). Crossing the line? A qualitative exploration of ICF master certified: Coaches' perception of roles, borders and boundaries. *International Coaching Psychology Review, 13*(2), 46–61.

Sinclair, L. (2021). *Mental health: These are the 10 types of overthinking to look out for, according to an expert.* Stylist. https://www.stylist.co.uk/health/mental-health/types-of-overthinking-expert-instagram/642450

Strevens, C., Field, R., & James, C. (2023). An analysis of studies on the wellbeing of law teachers in the UK and Australia in 2020 using the lens of seven psychosocial hazards of academic work. In *Wellbeing and the legal academy* (pp. 21–38). Springer International Publishing.

The Wellbeing Lab. (2021). 2019–2022 workplace report. AHRI. https://www.ahri.com.au/wp-content/uploads/MMcQ_WellbeingLab_Australia_WorkplaceSurvey_2019-2022-1.pdf

Trinca, H. (2022a, March 25). No silver bullet for a weary workforce after COVID. *The Australian.*

Trinca, H. (2022b, March 25). Companies need to "fix" work, not their workers, says Westpac's mental health leader. *The Australian.*

Trinca, H. (2023, April 14). Worker's compensation claims a threat to employers post-Covid. *The Australian.*

Unmind. (2022a). *7 trends that will shape workplace mental health in 2022.* Unmind. https://resources.unmind.com/7-trends-that-will-shape-workplace-mental-health-in-2022

Unmind. (2022b). *The great big burnout handbook: what it is (and isn't), why it's happening, and how to stop it for good.* Unmind. https://resources.unmind.com/the-great-big-burnout-handbook

Wray, S., & Kinman, G. (2022). The psychosocial hazards of academic work: An analysis of trends. *Studies in Higher Education, 47*(4), 771–782.

Chapter 2

Positive Wellbeing Within Workspaces

Angela R. Dobele and Lisa Farrell

Introduction

While there is no single accepted definition of wellbeing the Oxford English Dictionary defines it as:

> Wellbeing [noun] – the state of being comfortable, healthy or happy.[1]

What is particularly interesting about this definition is the use of the word comfortable. To improve wellbeing, the typical approach is to consider health (physical and mental) and happiness. The lack of attention given to being comfortable in the wellbeing literature has led to less focus on the physical aspects of our environment that can impact on our wellbeing. Given so much of our lives are spent at work, aspects of the workplace that impact our comfort levels is important to understand.

COVID-19 has redefined the physical workplace as academics have embraced working from home. Working from home is not new to academia, where periods of isolated work represent typical behaviours (e.g., research or writing-related activities). While terms like telecommuting and telework have been around for a while; however, the notion of completely working from home or maintaining a hybrid climate where teaching and teaching-related activities (including student consultations), peer collaborations and administrative tasks, including meetings, are all facilitated within the home environment, was new to many. However, we managed our workloads from home, simply because we had to and there seemed to be a consensus that people were productive (even more productive) when working from home (Lederman, 2022).

Nevertheless, the post-COVID world has reembraced the campus experience, deemed an important move for students, suggesting that the switch to online classes further exacerbated a variety of mental health issues (see Akpinar, 2021, for a summary). On campus tertiary activities include those designed to improve and support student wellbeing, including those designed to strengthen and support belonging and competence. Previous research has considered academic greenspaces and their impact on wellbeing, university performance and educational outcomes (Foellmer et al., 2021; Liu et al., 2022).

DOI: 10.4324/9781003284772-4

While a focus on holistic student experiences is important, a focus on staff wellbeing is too. There is increasing evidence of the positive correlation between greenspace and wellbeing (Conniff & Craig, 2016; Houlden et al., 2018). Thus, the University environment is important to the Higher Education staff experience. Greenspaces can be considered from the domains of building capacities (for example, in terms of facilitating social cohesion) or for their restorative capabilities (for example, physiological stress recovery) (as outlined in detail in Markevych et al., 2017).

Academic wellbeing is an important, timely and global issue. Sushok and Matson (2021) suggest that "higher education should lead the wellbeing revolution" (p. 1). What it means to be an academic now is difficult to understand (Archer, 2008; Rosewell & Ashwin, 2019). The result of these "new times" in "contemporary academia is increased pressures for performance and production" and "arguably, as likely to engender feelings of anxiety and inauthenticity, especially among 'older' and/or more senior academics" (Archer, 2008, p. 401). In this chapter, we focus initially on enhancing workplace comfort in academic work environments. The importance of comfort in workplaces is well recognised but usually focuses on physical comfort. In this chapter, we expand the concept to also include psychological comfort, often thought of as a sense of belonging, being connected or being supported (Lin, 1986).

As academics with a collective experience of 50 years in academia (16 in leadership roles of many types) across multiple countries we will reflect on our experiences of initiatives that supported workplace wellbeing through enhancing comfort. To undertake this task, we will employ a reflective practice methodology. In this way, we sought to understand similarities, differences, and patterns more deeply in our experiences, actions, and observations.

Workplace comfort matters as poor quality environments can lead to poor health resulting in lower productivity and absenteeism (i.e., Bubonya et al., 2017; Hilton et al., 2008; Johns, 2011). Estimates have shown that the payback for investments to improve indoor environmental quality (IEQ) of workplaces is generally less than two years (Wargocki et al., 2006) in terms of the financial value from the health and productivity benefits.

Reflection Methodology

Undertaking reflective practices helps to understand experiences or actions and provide a way forward in a process of continuous learning. Reflective analysis is a recognised research methodology (e.g., Cathro et al., 2017). Previous research has highlighted that reflection is an important activity for professional development (Clarà, 2015; Postholm, 2008), a key contributor of job satisfaction (Postholm & Wæge, 2016), and an important practice for co-leaders (Atieno Okech, 2008). Traditionally, reflective practice has occurred from the student side or focuses on teachers using it to benefit students.

The adoption of reflective research in this chapter responds to calls for global attention around the topic of academic wellbeing (Muurlink & Poyatos Matas, 2011) and the lack of data around the unique challenges and opportunities that online faculty face (Perrotta & Bohan, 2020). Importantly, the focus of reflection is positive forward-looking, rather than getting "stuck on … past experiences" (Postholm, 2009, p. 553). Given that we are interested in what works and how to improve academic wellbeing, this is a perfect lens. In reflection research, the aim is to think critically and consider the opportunities for change and advancement while being mindful of the broader considerations or assumptions that framed past courses of action (e.g., Brookfield, 1998).

In this chapter, we critically reflect on lived experiences, innovations and research projects, which have links to aspects of comfort in the academic work environments and the resultant/perceived impact on wellbeing. We review our experiences and practices through two complementary lenses, first, the academic leader as a reflective practitioner or self-assessor, and second the theoretical (indoor environment quality) lens applied to give structure to the examples we reflect on. In doing so, we began our reflections with consideration of comfort in the workplace followed by comfort in the working from home environment.

In each case, we reflected on aspects of both physical and psychological comfort. Reflections were developed using a structured narrative approach to reveal insights (Bruner, 2009; Polkinghorne, 1988) and took the form of written artefacts in which we recorded our thoughts and impressions as well as recording what we did or observed (Silverman & Marvasti, 2008). We considered how problems were solved and the resultant impact. Care was undertaken to ensure an ethical reflection, incorporating values within our critical thinking approach, including completing an ethics self-evaluation form provided by our review body for our approach. We would also note that we do not intend the strategies in this article as a substitute for the help of qualified professionals. We provide our reflections and seek to encourage conversations around potentially "useful coping tools for preventing and mitigating common struggles associated with academia" (Johnson & Lester, 2022, p. 10).

Workplace Comfort

It's estimated that people spend on average 87% of their time indoors, so this alone suggests that the quality of our spaces matters (Klepeis et al., 2001). Moreover, for those in the workforce many of these hours are spent in workplace buildings. In terms of academics, many of these builds are old (often of historical significance), aging or new and purpose built. But most are designed with student learning and pedagogy at the forefront rather than the needs of the academic staff who inhabit them on a day-to-day basis (Leijon et al., 2022). Therefore, they are not always optimal spaces for academics to work and engage in all the requirements of their roles (typically, teaching, research, and administration). Often older university buildings are partially retrofitted, and this can also be problematic (Zuhaib et al., 2018). Most of the research relating to IEQ is in the built environment literature and the focus is on aspects of IEQ that are easily measured and legally controlled (i.e., thermal, acoustic, visual and air quality properties) with a focus on how they impact physical health.

A review by Arif et al. (2016) also spoke to the tensions between Green-building principles, economic factors and IEQ. For example, hard materials for ease of cleaning can conflict with the acoustic comfort of the building's occupants. They conclude that the Green builds are not necessarily comfortable buildings and building design needs to factor in both sustainability and comfort factors with a need for monitoring once a building is occupied.

More recent literature has begun to consider the psychosocial comfort of buildings (e.g., Ortiz & Bluyssen, 2022). Employee comfort matters as it has been shown to impact on productivity and job satisfaction. Franke and Nadler (2021) conclude that there is the potential to increase the productivity of academic and professional support staff through improved IEQ in a study of a university building. Poor environments lead to poor physical and mental health that has indirect costs through absenteeism as well as the direct productivity losses. It is therefore in both the employers' and employees' interest to ensure workplaces are comfortable and hence wellbeing enhancing.

Reflections on Higher Education IEQ Comfort Initiatives

In our reflections, we recalled examples of wellbeing initiatives that we have been connected to or experienced in relation to IQE factors. We found that those which were memorable could be classified under two IEQ headings: (i) Sensory comfort and (ii) Psychosocial comfort.

Sensory Comfort

Example 1: Luminosity and Visual Discomfort – Natural Daylight Lamps

The importance of lighting on mental health has been well documented. For a review of the literature on luminosity and building comfort, see Galasiu and Veitch (2006) who conclude that employees have a strong preference for natural daylight. To enhance visual comfort, Lisa recalled her experience at first arriving as a Discipline Head to a city centre office block that had been repurposed to house academics and where many of the staff had internal offices that were deprived of any natural light. Moreover, external office with windows were allocated to more senior staff and so a hierarchical culture was imposed. The introduction of natural light, even if artificially created, is an important solution to enhance visual wellbeing especially in academia where long hours are spent reading and working on computers.

> My solution was to install natural day light lamps into the internal offices and the gratitude from staff was immense. They felt listened to, they felt valued. (LF reflection notes)

Additional to luminosity, a seminal study by Wells (1965) showed a preference for both daylight and an outdoor view. Lisa reflected on a further initiative in her building of dark windowless corridors in the form of the introduction of large art works, many of which were scenic. The effect of nature on wellbeing is well documented (e.g., Pritchard et al., 2020; Shanahan et al., 2019). Lisa recalled that this allowed for interaction between staff and visual stimulation as staff moved around the building. The effect of art on wellbeing is also well documented (see, for example, Lankston et al., 2010).

> The department also invested in artwork which was placed along the dark internal corridors and the building started to come out of the dark and into the light. The net result was staff were more likely to come to the office for their focused research time and to spend longer in the workplace. Moreover, I believe the culture slowly shifted to being less hierarchical and more inclusive with happier, more engaged, and brighter, staff. (LF reflection notes)

Example 2: Acoustic Discomfort – Pop-Up Quiet Spaces

Sensory overload is documented workplace environmental stressor (Baker, 1984) and previous research has considered the impact of this on productivity. The rise in employees diagnosed with sensory disorders and those who are neurodivergent also means more individuals are prone to sensory discomfort. Anderson et al. (2018) report on the high failure rate of sensory impacted students in higher education. Although there are multiple examples of workplace buildings with de-sensory spaces (often called quiet rooms), these are less common in higher education workplaces – often due to a lack of space in buildings. The obvious quiet space on campus is the library, but even libraries can struggle with noise-related issues. For a higher education library intervention study see McCaffrey and Breen (2016).

As a Head of Discipline, Lisa reported she was aware that academics were stressed in the busy noisy office environment with a combination of traditional offices, open plan and hot desks used by sessional and research staff. The academics talked of a need for a quiet space for focused work frequently. Naturally, the first consideration of a quiet space is of sound and lighting aspects. As a result, a pilot project was set up with the aim of creating a pop-up quiet space that could be moved across locations as spaces became available. The project team created a pop-up room kit bag which allowed the room to be packed up and transported across locations. So, it was not so much about the physical space, which was flexible, but what the space offered to participants.

> While the idea was to have a moveable kit that could be set up wherever space was available, finding free space was challenging. This meant that the quiet room was frequently relocating. This allowed us to establish proof of concept that it is possible to create a portable quiet space kit bag. Interestingly, those who used the room reported back that they used it to take time out rather than undertake focused work. It became a wellbeing space more than a quiet workspace. (LF reflection notes)

During our reflections, we realised that our typical leadership go-to solution was not appropriate for the quiet space room. The first response to the offering of the room to staff was to encourage its use, much the same as we would for any new building service. But sending out staff-all emails or repeated mentions at departmental meetings could have been confronting. There needs to be respect around potential

Table 2.1 The Pop-Up Wellbeing Kit Bag

While guides to building sensory rooms are common, the novelty of the pop-up space approach is that the items can fit into a kit bag and be easily moved across locations. Such an approach crystallises the focus on a wellbeing space rather than a sensory space.

Pop-up wellbeing kit bags can include:

- For visual comfort, a small lamp to provide soft lighting.
- Reading for relaxation and awareness (self-help) therapeutic/ self-help reading materials, for example, newspapers/magazines.
- Mindfulness activities such as adult colouring books and colouring pencils/pens.
- Small plant for air quality and aesthetic purposes.
- Connecting to nature and the outdoor environment using scenic prints/posters (that can be easily rolled up).
- Thermal comfort supports, for example, cushions and (weighted) blankets.

concerns, including associated stigmas. Overall, the room became well received because it provided a hidey hole in which to work uninterrupted. But accessing it became more of a process of word-of-mouth, led by Lisa, rather than that of more "official" institutional communication.

Further reflections on the room's contents encouraged Lisa and her team to rethink the contents of the quiet room kit bag and adapt it to a wellbeing space kit bag. Table 2.1 is a summary of those reflections and other items could also be added depending on the wellbeing practices of the users, such as a rollout yoga mat.

In this way, sensitive thought is given to flexible design considerations and inclusivity and responds to the need for guidance around quiet space design (Sadia, 2020). During reflection, Lisa realised that a key element of quiet spaces is not restricted to design elements, although these are important. Of equal importance is the process by which staff can access and utilise these spaces and the role that users play in the design, such that inclusivity is paramount.

Example 3:.Acoustic Discomfort – Shut Up and Write

Permitting natural light to flow through a building often results in open plan spaces, but open plan spaces suffer from noise pollution (Passero & Zannin, 2012; Pierrette et al., 2015; Roskams et al., 2019). Thus, there is tension between light and sound when considering building design. Office noise has been shown to lead to employee stress (Johnson, 1991) and negatively impact workplace and environmental satisfaction, and job performance (Göçer et al., 2019; Sundstrom et al., 1994).

Angela reflected on her running Shut Up and Write sessions through the lens of acoustic discomfort. Shut Up and Write sessions are group writing sessions that allow academics focused quiet time to complete papers and other written tasks in a supportive group environment (e.g., Fegan, 2016; Mewburn et al., 2014; O'Dwyer et al., 2016). Shut Up and Write groups provide space for dedicated writing and skills development in a supportive environment (O'Dwyer et al., 2017). Angela realised that such groups allowed for acoustic relief. For example, when the sessions were held in an on-campus board or meeting room, with or without background music or held in a local café. Participants could focus in the presence of other participants who were all silent and writing. The noise of keyboard keys tapping or pens on paper provided a focal point.

> What was interesting was noticing colleagues who said they found it difficult to focus for 25 minutes at a stretch, getting into the rhythms of writing during our sessions. Our starting timer would make a ticking noise and an alarm sounds at the end of the 25 minutes. Sometimes, we'd become so engrossed in our writing that the finish alarm would startle us. I realised that our daily lives are pretty noisy. (ARD reflection notes)

In further reflections, Angela began to realise a secondary benefit of her writing groups: the witnessing of the importance of collegiality and support. The higher education industry has become an increasingly competitive and commodified environment. Academics must publish or perish, competing against each other for grants, publications acceptances, good teaching scores and media and community attentions. Badri summarises the current situation, "With more work-related demands and due to the importance of work as a critical source for human survival, people cannot help themselves from being bounded with the vicious cycle of work" (Badri, 2019, p. 226). Such a hypercompetitive culture has given rise to the term "dark academia" (Fleming, 2019, p. 2) and an increased focus on wellbeing health in academia (Johnson & Lester, 2022).

COVID-19 has further exacerbated these stresses with "pandemic burnout" now said to be "rampant in academia" (Gewin, 2021, p. 489). Access to social supports, including peer networks, may help, through job stress mitigation (Nicholls et al., 2022). Our periods of individual reflection highlighted the shared realisation of the importance of our peers. ARD summarises as follows:

> Over a decade or so of running Shut Up and Write groups, I realised there are deeper, more personal benefits, over and above achieving writing goals, including outputs. Staff are part of a social and cohesive group. I've seen motivation levels, academic confidence and positive feelings towards writing returned or increased. Writing in the company of others helped reduce alienation, feeling like writing is a lonely endeavour or wondering if their feelings and experiences were unique. What I realised, is that the sessions provided a physical space to complete the work, but also a mental space to focus on that work. (ARD reflection notes)

Academic isolation and emotional vulnerability have been shown to have increased during COVID-19 (Haas et al., 2020; Morley & Aston, 2023), and although the focus has mostly been on students (e.g., Haas et al., 2020; Morley & Aston, 2023), writing groups and Shut Up and Write sessions can develop and maintain a sense of academic community in a fragmented world (Boix et al., 2021; Halcomb, 2021; Morley & Aston, 2023). In running online writing groups during COVID-19 work from home requirements, Angela realised, once again, the potential for therapeutic benefits and noticed that the building of these social supports formed an important part of self-care.

> I found the opportunity to communicate informally with staff around the shut up and write sessions to be useful. We were all in this situation together, and tips and tricks were often offered in this virtual but still friendly and social environment. Then, when we got down to writing, the support was focussed on the work, which helped to maintain motivation. Sometimes the latest news made it hard to focus, and we would open the writing session with a discussion, but then, when the timer started…well, I think we felt like it was okay that we put those troubles down for a bit, that the worry and noise in our heads could be permissively silenced, and we could get back into the topics we enjoy researching and teaching. It was a nice feeling, being able to get back to those topics. (ARD reflection notes)

With this example, Angela realised that the writing groups provided a buffer for the academic stress and isolation we feel, especially during the significantly changed times of COVID-19.

Example 4: Air Quality and Olfactory Discomfort – Food Odours

While there is literature that relates comfort to air quality (see for example, Derbez et al., 2014; Ma et al., 2021) the focus here tends to be on the composition of the air such as the levels of carbon dioxide, temperature, relative humidity etc. A common worker complaint in offices relates to odours and olfactory discomfort is noted in the literature (see, for example, Frontczak & Wargocki, 2011; Šenitková, 2017). Moreover, for some individuals this can be a significant issue. In open place office spaces smells easily propagate, yet controlled building ventilation systems mean that it is often not possible to open windows to clear unpleasant odours quickly and effectively.

Angela reflected on complaints from staff regarding this issue in relation to food odours from kitchen and ancillary areas and people eating at their desks in open plan areas.

> We had a regular lunch time quiz in one of the main staff rooms and the table was full, it was a lovely atmosphere, with a little bit of friendly competition. Another member of staff heated their fish dish and the room exploded with a very strong smell. A vegetarian member of staff had to leave. Some of the staff in the area came to speak with me. It's a difficult issue. Some people are really sensitive to aromas of all kinds. Yes, we could say an empathetic colleague might not bring in "smelly" foods, or respond favourably to a discussion on staff room etiquette, but I felt we couldn't ban food types and call ourselves inclusive. (ARD reflection notes)

Such complaints are difficult to deal with in highly controlled buildings. Although there is a move to allow building occupants better control over the thermal aspects of their indoor environment (Ma et al., 2021), building design is yet to address this source of discomfort effectively. But building design and wellbeing go hand in glove, albeit with further research required (see Hanc et al., 2019, for a conceptual review). In our reflections, the need to raise awareness of the issue was discussed, with the twin goals of being empathetic to others and respectful of the diverse workplace that represented our institution. These occurred in conjunction with being smarter about building usage, such as considering where the microwave ovens will be located and putting in closable doors if required. However, given the experiences of the University of Canberra library, perhaps we do need to consider banning durian.

Psychosocial Comfort

Example 1: Inclusivity – The Women's Wall

Academic environments and buildings often struggle to be inclusive. Factors affecting people's perception of the psychosocial comfort of a space are often a function of the way the building is decorated, which includes the use of notice boards and the nature of the works of art hanging on the walls, etc. Buildings that reflect the cultural and collective meaning of their occupants offer greater levels of comfort (Heerwagen & Heerwagen, 2017). If we cannot identify with a space, then it is hard to connect to that space. Social exclusion is known for its impact on wellbeing and links to depression, productivity, and absenteeism (Appau et al., 2019; Lerner & Henke, 2008).

In this context, Lisa noted that almost every academic building has a notice board as you enter each academic department, filled with the front page of research papers of the department staff. Interestingly, these are nearly always from the older white male academics. To address this inequity with regards to gender, Lisa introduced a Women's Wall to provide a space for women to showcase their achievements. This resulted in an increase in the awareness of the contribution to the department made by the female academics. It made the female staff feel valued and was a useful vehicle in changing the culture of her workplace, fostering better recognition and respect for the female academics among themselves and their male colleagues.

> Sometimes we just need to experiment to see what works. This is a perfect example of an experiment that gained momentum and recognition and links to a growing set of ideas about the impact that the items we place on the walls in our working environments impacts our perceptions of inclusion and safety within these environments. (LF reflection notes)

Lisa went on to cite the example of Harvard University Portraiture Project that is changing the portraits hanging on the university's walls to be more inclusive of gender and race[2]. The project aims to create an environment in which a more diverse societal group can feel a sense of belonging.

Angela felt that the Women's Wall was a wonderful signal for "You can't be what you can't see" (Grimshaw, 2022, p. 10), as it offered different role models and examples of academic achievement. She further reflected:

> What the Women's Wall accomplished was to signal achievements beyond A*
> publications. It highlighted teaching, leadership, and community outcomes as
> well. It was right there, on the wall, putting a spotlight on the many and varied

tasks being done by staff and done well. Lisa also offered alternative avenues for being featured, it wasn't restricted to self-nomination but also peer nominations. Which meant a way for staff to nominate the accomplishments of others, thereby giving voice to the humble, shy, and overlooked. (ARD reflection notes)

Lisa also noted that the wall later developed to include additional information, such as that related to economic labour, industry promotion and pay scale data, institutional strategy data and upcoming university events or initiatives that should be noted. Some of the benefits she witnessed from showcasing staff achievements included engagement, peer praise and visibility. However, something to note for such initiatives is the need to have recognised responsibility for the space. There needs to be a timely rotation and updating of the information featured.

Example 2: Psychological Buffers – Meeting Free February/Slowdown Weeks

While buildings designed for wellbeing should facilitate social interaction and places for coming together, office cultures that are excessive in terms of formal meetings can be challenging for workers. (Polzer & DeFilippis, 2020; Villinski, 2016). Many psychological factors triggered by building design impact workplace productivity. For example, in open plan environments with central meeting rooms designated by glass partitions, there is an incentive for workers to be seen in meetings even if those meetings might not be the most productive use of time, and often meeting rooms are overused due to concerns for speech privacy in open plan environments (Acun & Yilmazer, 2018; Sundstrom et al., 1982).

Psychological buffers can help build resilience to the factors that trigger poor productivity and give an employee a sense of control over these factors. A psychological buffer is a process in which a psychosocial resource is employed to reduce the impact of a source of stress on a person's psychological wellbeing. In relation to academia, many academics suffer from stress-related issues (Winefield, 2003). For Lisa, the psychological trigger for exhaustion was an excessive meeting schedule following an intensive round of strategic planning meetings. Hence, she implemented a self-intervention she called Meeting Free February. Meeting fatigue is a phenomenon that occurs when a high frequency of meetings impacts on an employee's motivation and hence productivity.

In my case, meeting fatigue set in after a long round of strategic planning for the next year, when I noted that I was feeling impatient in meetings. For example, when meetings were running late, I caught myself wanting to repeatedly look at my watch. When discussions became side-tracked, I became frustrated, wanting to redirect the meetings back to the stated agenda. (LF reflection notes)

A workplace culture of frequent meetings can result in employees feeling like the meetings are a waste of their time and affect their level of engagement with their roles, ultimately impacting on their productivity. The purpose of Meeting Free February was to allow Lisa a month free from face-to-face meetings to create a psychological buffer for the rest of the year.

In general, the hypothesis that it was possible to engineer a break from meetings while remaining productive and delivering on the requirements of my role was proven for me. This was empowering and motivating. (LF reflection notes)

Reflecting on what she learnt from the intervention Lisa stated:

Meeting Free February allowed me to experiment with alternatives to holding traditional meetings and built my confidence to question the need and purpose of a meeting and my abilities to offer a different way to conduct the business associated with my role. (LF reflection notes)

Although the location of meetings has certainly changed in the post-COVID-19 environment, this has not necessarily reduced the number of meetings. In fact, a whole new psychological phenomenon of Team and Zoom fatigue was born (e.g., Nesher Shoshan & Wehrt, 2022). As Angela reflects:

I realised that online meetings were scheduled back-to-back, and because I was sitting at my home desk there were few opportunities for breaks between these meetings. Even a few minutes spent walking from one room to another provided a short respite. Sometimes, our on campus meetings were in different buildings, so it was a chance to get outside, experience weather, admire a flowering tree, perhaps walk via a café and grab a drink on the way. I hadn't realised how important these micro-breaks between the meetings were to me, until they were gone. (ARD reflection notes)

The ease of online meetings in many instances increased their frequency and many things that could have been decided outside of a meeting by default become an online meeting. Added to these stressors was the loss of demarcation lines between home and work. All these factors can impact on wellbeing.

Our university created a slowdown week period, held in the mid-semester break. No formal institutional meetings, institutional events or seminars are scheduled. Staff and students are notified in advance and the requirements for timely email replies are relaxed during this week. By implementing a set period for being meeting free or having such an institutionally endorsed lead period of time, staff are provided with a psychological wellbeing buffer. In our experience, these buffers were very welcome; perhaps because you know it is coming, it helps provide the energy needed to keep going in the busier times. The need for psychological buffers remains real.

Example 3: Belonging – Personalised Spaces and Dedicated Home Office Workspaces

Heerwagen and Orians (1986) showed, in a university-based study, that employees in windowless environments put up more visual materials to compensate for the lack of visual stimulation in their indoor environment. Previous research has considered

Table 2.2 Working Space Personalisation Ideas

Personalising our working spaces can help us feel more comfortable in the space. Allowing staff such freedoms can help promote collaboration, a sense of belonging and positively impact wellbeing. In a climate of shared offices, open planning and hot desking, these are important considerations. Personalised items can be small and portable, including digital personalisations, or more permanent.
Personalised work spaces might include:

- Water fountains or other sound or white noise generators.
- Playing background noises such as music, café sounds or other ambience choices that resonate.
- Photographs, pictures, wall hangings and posters (these could hold meaning or connection, such as a loved one's photograph, or remind us of overseas travels or a different time).
- Decorations, mementoes and accessories (again, these could hold meaning or connection (including plants, figurines, cushion for office chair and toys).
- Lamps (there is a huge variety of lamps on the market, think about the lighting options (e.g., dimming) and also what else they can offer (e.g., decorative (e.g., Tiffany, creative or Banker, Lava or light show lamps, vitamin D or terrarium or hydroponic enabling).
- Desk fan to circulate the air and provide white noise.
- Personalised technology (laptop cases or machine top, screensavers).
- Personalised workstation resources (such as hanging a bright jacket or hat from the coatrack or a bright vest over the back of the office chair).

the organisation and arrangement of a "productive" office (e.g., Harris, 2019; Zamani & Gum, 2019), including for specific productivity outputs, such as academic writing (Dobele & Veer, 2019). As Angela summarises:

Years ago, my Mum gave me a small water fountain. It has sat next to my office desk ever since. I found the trickling water noise to be very soothing. It helps me block out other noises. Plus, looking at the waterfall when I'm having a writer's block moment has helped me find the words or regain my train of my thought. It's a lovely thing to have in my office, I find it peaceful. (ARD reflection notes)

This is one example of staff personalising their workspaces with the aim of enhancing their wellbeing. Table 2.2 provides other examples that we either use or have observed.

Previous research has considered the link between employee wellbeing and interior space and office landscape (e.g., Colenberg et al., 2021; Cordero et al., 2019). Personalising our working spaces offers an opportunity to impact our mood, sense of belonging, creativity, productivity and happiness (e.g., Groen et al., 2019; Hunter, 2022). The impacts can be profound and we can achieve personalisations on any budget. We are limited only by our imagination and perhaps a little trial and error to determine what works for us.

Conclusion

Our workspaces impact on wellbeing in real and impactful ways. In this chapter, we considered the important characteristics of academic workspace and how these can impact on our sensory and psychosocial comfort. While building design has focused on comfort-related issues, our approach was to apply a wellbeing lens to this relationship. Comfort is an essential element of high levels of wellbeing. Through a reflections methodology, we have been able to highlight innovations and initiatives from our collective 50 years of lived experience as academics.

We have highlighted the things that worked, although not all perfectly or quite as expected, in the hope that others might follow by implementing some of the schemes noted or be courageous to try something new to improve the comfort of themselves or others in the academic workplace. Importantly, the examples reflected on offer a range of ideas that can be implemented from an individual, school/department, college/faculty, and University level. Wellbeing support occurs at all these levels, and it is everyone's responsibility to be mindful of their wellbeing and the wellbeing of their work colleagues.

Reflections from Chapter Authors

Being familiar with reflective discourses, we still found the emotional side of this process for this chapter to be interesting, and challenging. The modern world of academia has challenges, and they need to be addressed. Some of these were exacerbated during COVID-19, when we worked from home, taught from home, researched from home, conducted our meetings and social engagements from home. Others have been brought to the surface in the growing wake of higher education colleagues and peers leaving the profession, experiencing challenges to their wellbeing and the rising instances we see of exhaustion and stress and anxiety. High turnover is becoming the norm, and the resulting brain drain as these talented staff leave the profession is a serious risk in a knowledge-based industry. You're probably seeing it, too.

When we worked from home, many of us created welcoming and productive spaces. We tried to be kind to ourselves and each other in those home-based spaces. If we are to encourage, and meaningfully support a return to work ethos, the workplace has to be attractive. We now understand that it needs to entice staff through a welcoming space, one that can nurture relationships and be conducive to both productivity and sustained wellbeing. Our experiences are that security in the higher education industry has eroded, and with that erosion, the support one can gain from

Figure 2.1 Reflection Drawing – A Supportive Workplace Nurtures and Empowers Employee Wellbeing

Source: Original drawing by Margaret McLuckie, used with permission.

the workplace becomes paramount to attracting new hires and retaining quality employees. The workplace needs to empower employees (as reflected in our drawing, Figure 2.1).

In all our years of being academics, what we see around us is increasing levels of extreme unwellness. And that concerns us – for our colleagues and ourselves. In a knowledge society, is it those most able that enter the profession. Today, we face the serious concern that the most talented no longer see academia as a credible career option.

We worry for both early-career academics entering this profession, and for current colleagues and peers. Although we are nostalgic for academia as it once was, we are realistic enough to realise that going back is not possible. What is needed is a better way forward. We believe the time for change is now.

Notes

1 Oxford Dictionaries, Oxford University Press (2016) Retrieved April 01, 2023, from http://www.oxforddictionaries.com/
2 The Portraiture Project, Harvard University Office for Equity, Diversity, Inclusion, and Belonging: The Portraiture Project | The Harvard Foundation. Retrieved April 01, 2023

References

Acun, V., & Yilmazer, S. (2018). A grounded theory approach to investigate the perceived soundscape of open-plan offices. *Applied Acoustics, 131*, 28–37.

Akpınar, E. (2021). The effect of online learning on tertiary level students mental health during the COVID-19 lockdown. *The European Journal of Social & Behavioural Sciences, 30*(1), 52–63.

Anderson, A. H., Carter, M., & Stephenson, J. (2018). Perspectives of university students with autism spectrum disorder. *Journal of Autism and Developmental Disorders, 48*, 651–665.

Appau, S., Churchill, S. A., & Farrell, L. (2019). Social integration and subjective wellbeing. *Applied Economics, 51*(16), 1748–1761.

Archer, L. (2008). Younger academics' constructions of "authenticity", "success" and professional identity. *Studies in Higher Education, 33*(4), 385–403.

Arif, M., Katafygiotou, M., Mazroei, A., Kaushik, A., & Elsarrag, E. (2016). Impact of indoor environmental quality on occupant well-being and comfort: A review of the literature. *International Journal of Sustainable Built Environment, 5*(1), 1–11.

Atieno Okech, J. E. (2008). Reflective practice in group co-leadership. *The Journal for Specialists in Group Work, 33*(3), 236–252.

Badri, S. (2019). Affective well-being in the higher education sector: Connecting work-life balance with mental health, job satisfaction and turnover intention issues inside the academia setting. *International Journal of Happiness and Development, 5*(3), 225–241.

Baker, C. F. (1984). Sensory overload and noise in the ICU: Sources of environmental stress. *Critical Care Nursing Quarterly, 6*(4), 66–80.

Boix, V., Lindström, J., Löfgreen, J., Månefjord, H., Pettersson, M., & von Platten, J. (2021, December 9). *The LU PhD writing lab: Helping PhD students build effective and sustainable writing habits, one writing snack at a time.* LTHs 11: e pedagogiska inspirationskonferens [Conference]. Lund University, Lund, Sweden.

Brookfield, S. (1998). Critically reflective practice. *Journal of Continuing Education in the Health Professions, 18*(4), 197–205.

Bruner, J. S. (2009). *Actual minds, possible worlds.* Harvard University Press.

Bubonya, M., Cobb-Clark, D. A., & Wooden, M. (2017). Mental health and productivity at work: Does what you do matter? *Labour Economics, 46*, 150–165.

Cathro, V., O'Kane, P., & Gilbertson, D. (2017). Assessing reflection: Understanding skill development through reflective learning journals. *Education + Training, 59*(4), 427–442.

Clarà, M. (2015). What is reflection? Looking for clarity in an ambiguous notion. *Journal of Teacher Education, 66*(3), 261–271.

Colenberg, S., Jylhä, T., & Arkesteijn, M. (2021). The relationship between interior office space and employee health and well-being – a literature review. *Building Research & Information, 49*(3), 352–366.

Conniff, A., & Craig, T. (2016). A methodological approach to understanding the wellbeing and restorative benefits associated with greenspace. *Urban Forestry & Urban Greening, 19*, 103–109.

Cordero, A. C., Babapour, M., & Karlsson, M. (2019). Feel well and do well at work: A post-relocation study on the relationships between employee wellbeing and office landscape. *Journal of Corporate Real Estate, 22*(2), 113–137.

Derbez, M., Berthineau, B., Cochet, V., Lethrosne, M., Pignon, C., Riberon, J., & Kirchner, S. (2014). Indoor air quality and comfort in seven newly built, energy-efficient houses in France. *Building and Environment, 72*, 173–187.

Dobele, A. R., & Veer, E. (2019). My best writing space: Understanding academics self-professed writing spaces. *Higher Education, 78*, 345–364.

Fegan, S. (2016). When shutting up brings us together: Several affordances of a scholarly writing group. *Journal of Academic Language and Learning, 10*(2), A20–A31.

Fleming, P. (2019). Dark academia: Despair in the neoliberal business school. *Journal of Management Studies, 57*(6), 1305–1311.

Foellmer, J., Kistemann, T., & Anthonj, C. (2021). Academic greenspace and well-being—can campus landscape be therapeutic? Evidence from a German university. *Wellbeing, Space and Society, 2*, 100003.

Franke, M., & Nadler, C. (2021). Towards a holistic approach for assessing the impact of IEQ on satisfaction, health, and productivity. *Building Research & Information, 49*(4), 417–444.

Frontczak, M., & Wargocki, P. (2011). Literature survey on how different factors influence human comfort in indoor environments. *Building and Environment, 46*(4), 922–937.

Galasiu, A. D., & Veitch, J. A. (2006). Occupant preferences and satisfaction with the luminous environment and control systems in daylit offices: A literature review. *Energy Build, 38(7),* 728e42.

Gewin, V. (2021). Pandemic burnout is rampant in academia. *Nature, 591*(7850), 489–492.

Göçer, Ö, Candido, C., Thomas, L., & Göçer, K. (2019). Differences in occupants' satisfaction and perceived productivity in high-and low-performance offices. *Buildings, 9*(9), 199.

Grimshaw, M. (2022). You can't be what you can't see! *Primary Science, 174*, 10–12.

Groen, B., van der Voordt, T., Hoekstra, B., & van Sprang, H. (2019). Impact of employee satisfaction with facilities on self-assessed productivity support. *Journal of Facilities Management, 17*(5), 442–462.

Haas, S., De Soete, A., & Ulstein, G. (2020). Zooming through covid: Fostering safe communities of critical reflection via online writers' group interaction. *DOUBLE HELIX (HAMDEN), 8*, 1–11.

Halcomb, L. (2021). Strategies for becoming a successful writer. *Nurse Researcher, 29*(1), 5.

Hanc, M., McAndrew, C., & Ucci, M. (2019). Conceptual approaches to wellbeing in buildings: A scoping review. *Building Research & Information, 47*(6), 767–783.

Harris, R. (2019). Defining and measuring the productive office. *Journal of Corporate Real Estate, 21*(1), 55–71.

Heerwagen, J., & Heerwagen, J. H. (2017, June 6). Psychosocial value of space. *Whole Building Design Guide.* https://www.wbdg.org/resources/psychosocial-value-space?r=ieq

Heerwagen, J. H., & Orians, G. H. (1986). Adaptations to windowlessness: A study of the use of visual decor in windowed and windowless offices. *Environment and Behavior, 18*(5), 623–639.

Hilton, M. F., Scuffham, P. A., Sheridan, J., Cleary, C. M., & Whiteford, H. A. (2008). Mental ill-health and the differential effect of employee type on absenteeism and presenteeism. *Journal of Occupational and Environmental Medicine, 50*(11), 1228–1243.

Houlden, V., Weich, S., Porto de Albuquerque, J., Jarvis, S., & Rees, K. (2018). The relationship between greenspace and the mental wellbeing of adults: A systematic review. *PloS One, 13*(9), e0203000.

Hunter, C. (2022). Happy objects at work: the circulation of happiness. *Culture and Organization, 28*(2), 129–147.

Johns, G. (2011). Attendance dynamics at work: The antecedents and correlates of presenteeism, absenteeism, and productivity loss. *Journal of Occupational Health Psychology, 16*(4), 483.

Johnson, A. P., & Lester, R. J. (2022). Mental health in academia: Hacks for cultivating and sustaining wellbeing. *American Journal of Human Biology, 34*, e23664.

Johnson, D. (1991). Stress among graduates working in the SME sector. *Journal of Managerial Psychology, 6*(5), 17–21.

Klepeis, N. E., Nelson, W. C., Ott, W. R., Robinson, J. P., Tsang, A. M., Switzer, P., Behar, J. V., Hern, S. C., & Engelmann, W. H. (2001). The National Human Activity Pattern Survey (NHAPS): A resource for assessing exposure to environmental pollutants. *Journal of Exposure Science & Environmental Epidemiology, 11*(3), 231–252.

Lankston, L., Cusack, P., Fremantle, C., & Isles, C. (2010). Visual art in hospitals: Case studies and review of the evidence. *Journal of the Royal Society of Medicine, 103*(12), 490–499.

Lederman, D. (2022, January 04). The Era of Flexible Work in Higher Education, Administrators at two universities discuss their efforts to reimagine how, when and where their employees will work now and in the future. Inside Higher Ed. https://www.insidehighered.com/news/2022/01/05/era-flexible-work-higher-education-has-begun

Leijon, M., Nordmo, I., Tieva, Å, & Troelsen, R.. (2022). Formal learning spaces in higher Education–a systematic review. *Teaching in Higher Education, 29*(6), 1–22.

Lerner, D., & Henke, R. M. (2008). What does research tell us about depression, job performance, and work productivity? *Journal of Occupational and Environmental Medicine, 50*(4), 401–410.

Lin, N. (1986). Conceptualizing social support. *Social support, life events, and depression.* Elsevier, 17–30.

Liu, Q., Luo, S., Shen, Y., Zhu, Z., Yao, X., Li, Q., & Zhuo, Z. (2022). Relationships between students' demographic characteristics, perceived naturalness and patterns of use associated with campus green space, and self-rated restoration and health. *Urban Forestry & Urban Greening, 68*, 127474.

Markevych, I., Schoierer, J., Hartig, T., Chudnovsky, A., Hystad, P., Dzhambov, A. M., & Fuertes, E. (2017). Exploring pathways linking greenspace to health: Theoretical and methodological guidance. *Environmental Research, 158*, 301–317.

McCaffrey, C., & Breen, M. (2016). Quiet in the library: An evidence-based approach to improving the student experience. *Portal: Libraries and the Academy, 16*(4), 775–791.

Mewburn, I., Osborne, L., & Caldwell, G. A. (2014). Shut up and write! Some surprising uses of cafes and crowds in doctoral writing. *Writing Groups for Doctoral Education and Beyond: Innovations in Theory and Practice*, 399–425.

Morley, C., & Aston, S. (2023). Overcoming isolation with community based digital writing initiatives. *Journal of University Teaching and Learning Practice, 20*(2), 03.

Muurlink, O., & Poyatos Matas, C. (2011). A higher degree of stress: academic wellbeing. *Taking Wellbeing forward in higher education: Reflections on theory and practice*, 60–71.

Ma, N., Aviv, D., Guo, H., & Braham, W. W. (2021). Measuring the right factors: A review of variables and models for thermal comfort and indoor air quality. *Renewable and Sustainable Energy Reviews, 135*, 110436.

Nesher Shoshan, H., & Wehrt, W. (2022). Understanding "Zoom fatigue": A mixed-method approach. *Applied Psychology*, *71*(3), 827–852.

Nicholls, H., Nicholls, M., Tekin, S., Lamb, D., & Billings, J. (2022). The impact of working in academia on researchers' mental health and well-being: A systematic review and qualitative meta-synthesis. *PloS One*, *17*(5), e0268890.

O'Dwyer, S. T., McDonough, S. L., Jefferson, R., Goff, J. A., & Redman-MacLaren, M. (2017). Writing groups in the digital age: A case study analysis of shut up & write Tuesdays. In *Research 2.0 and the impact of digital technologies on scholarly inquiry* (pp. 249–269). IGI Global.

O'Dwyer, S. T., Jefferson, R., Goff, S. L. M. J. A., & Redman-MacLaren, M. (2016). Writing Groups in the Digital Age: A Case Study Analysis of Shut Up and Write Tuesdays. *Research 2.0 and the Impact of Digital Technologies on Scholarly Inquiry*. A. Esposito, 249–269.

Ortiz, M. A., & Bluyssen, P. M. (2022). Profiling office workers based on their self-reported preferences of indoor environmental quality and psychosocial comfort at their workplace during COVID-19. *Building and Environment*, *211*, 108742.

Passero, C. R. M., & Zannin, P. H. T. (2012). Acoustic evaluation and adjustment of an open-plan office through architectural design and noise control. *Applied Ergonomics*, *43*(6), 1066–1071.

Perrotta, K. A., & Bohan, C. H. (2020). A reflective study of online faculty teaching experiences in higher education. *Journal of Effective Teaching in Higher Education*, *3*(1), 50–66.

Pierrette, M., Parizet, E., Chevret, P., & Chatillon, J. (2015). Noise effect on comfort in open-space offices: Development of an assessment questionnaire. *Ergonomics*, *58*(1), 96–106.

Polkinghorne, D. E. (1988). *Narrative knowing and the human sciences*. Suny Press.

Polzer, J. T., & DeFilippis, E. (2020). The consequences of collaboration overload. *Academy of Management Proceedings*, 2020(1), 21045.

Postholm, M. B. (2008). Teachers developing practice: Reflection as key activity. *Teaching and Teacher Education*, *24*(7), 1717–1728.

Postholm, M. B. (2009). Research and development work: Developing teachers as researchers or just teachers? *Educational Action Research*, *17*(4), 551–565.

Postholm, M. B., & Wæge, K. (2016). Teachers' learning in school-based development. *Educational Research*, *58*(1), 24–38.

Pritchard, A., Richardson, M., Sheffield, D., & McEwan, K. (2020). The relationship between nature connectedness and eudaimonic well-being: A meta-analysis. *Journal of Happiness Studies*, *21*, 1145–1167.

Rosewell, K., & Ashwin, P. (2019). Academics' perceptions of what it means to be an academic. *Studies in Higher Education*, *44*(12), 2374–2384.

Roskams, M., Haynes, B., Lee, P. J., & Park, S. H. (2019). Acoustic comfort in open-plan offices: The role of employee characteristics. *Journal of Corporate Real Estate*, *21*(3), 254–270.

Sadia, T. (2020, December 21). Exploring the design preferences of neurodivergent populations for quiet spaces. Engineers engrxiv archive. https://doi.org/10.31224/osf.io/fkaqj

Šenitková, I. J. (2017). Indoor air quality and thermal comfort in school buildings. *IOP Conference Series: Earth and Environmental Science*, *95*(4), 042068. IOP Publishing.

Shanahan, D. F., Astell-Burt, T., Barber, E. A., Brymer, E., Cox, D. T., Dean, J., Depledge, M., Fuller, R. A., Hartig, T., & Irvine, K. N. (2019). Nature-based interventions for improving health and wellbeing: The purpose, the people and the outcomes. *Sports*, *7*(6), 141.

Sushok, F., & Matson, T. (2021). Why higher education should lead the wellbeing revolution. *Gallup Education, January*, *29*.

Silverman, D., & Marvasti, A. (2008). *Doing qualitative research: A comprehensive guide*, Sage.

Sundstrom, E., Herbert, R. K., & Brown, D. W. (1982). Privacy and communication in an open-plan office: A case study. *Environment and Behavior*, *14*(3), 379–392.

Sundstrom, E., Town, J. P., Rice, R. W., Osborn, D. P., & Brill, M. (1994). Office noise, satisfaction, and performance. *Environment and Behavior*, *26*(2), 195–222.

Villinski, A. P. (2016). Collaborative overload. *Harvard Business Review*.

Wargocki, P., Seppänen, O., Andersson, J., Clements-Croome, D., Fitzner, K., & Hanssen, S. (2006). Indoor climate and productivity in offices. *REHVA Guidebook*, *6*, 10–14.

Wells, B. W. P. (1965). Subjective responses to the lighting installations in a modern office building and their design implications. *Building and Environment*, *1*, 57–68.

Winefield, A. H. (2003). Stress in university academics. In *Occupational stress in the service professions* (pp. 251–274). CRC Press.

Zamani, Z., & Gum, D. (2019). Activity-based flexible office: Exploring the fit between physical environment qualities and user needs impacting satisfaction, communication, collaboration and productivity. *Journal of Corporate Real Estate*, *21*(3), 234–253.

Zuhaib, S., Manton, R., Griffin, C., Hajdukiewicz, M., Keane, M. M., & Goggins, J. (2018). An indoor environmental quality (IEQ) assessment of a partially-retrofitted university building. *Building and Environment*, *139*, 69–85.

Chapter 3

Provision of Wellbeing Services

Ekant Veer, Mona Soltani, and Tracey Robinson

Introduction

Most modern universities operate as small ecosystems akin to a village or, in some cases, a fully serviced town. Entertainment, medical care, food services, accommodation, professional development services, and childcare all sit alongside the core business functions of teaching and research at larger higher education institutions (Bromley, 2006). These units may be scattered around a town/city or co-located in a contained campus space. As a collective, these services are often dreamt to be a supportive, collaborative, accessible space that is open to staff and students alike. In reality, the co-location model is not so simple when it comes to addressing staff wellbeing.

There is no lack of evidence that shows that the wellbeing of staff is crucial for building a healthy and sustainable workforce (Abery & Gunson, n.d.; O'Brien & Guiney, 2018). Further to this, we know that the wellbeing of academics in higher education is declining (Lashuel, 2020; Mudrak et al., 2018; Taggart, 2021). Employee wellbeing, in general, and academic wellbeing, specifically, is central to creating an effective and engaging learning environment (Roos & Borkoski, 2021; Stuckey et al., 2019). As such, it is incumbent on employers to ensure their workplaces provide the appropriate services to support employees' wellbeing; however, determining how those services are offered is not necessarily an easy task.

Many authors, including those in this book, have explored multiple ways in which services can support the wellbeing of a workforce; however, the manner in which these services are made available and accessible to academics in universities comes with a myriad of problems. Determining how wellbeing services are accessed is particularly problematic when the stigma associated with mental health is still prevalent in many cultures and the desire to keep such issues private is commensurably prevalent. We are faced with a wicked problem where a solution may only lead to further undesired outcomes. Where a plethora of mental wellbeing services on campus may signal to some that the problem is being taken seriously without a culture that is accepting of normalising mental wellness, we could see services being avoided. That is, having physical access to services may not mean

DOI: 10.4324/9781003284772-5

that services are used when the stigma associated with mental wellbeing is still dominant in a workplace culture (Essential Elements of Organizational Initiatives to Improve Workplace Wellbeing, 2017; Spence, 2015).

This chapter explores the impact of services that are available physically on campus versus the unintended consequences that may accompany the use/available of such services. We offer an insight into the tensions that exist with various services (on-campus, off-campus, and online) and what impact each may have on developing support structures for academics at universities. We argue that ultimately, many of the issues associated with accessing mental wellbeing services on-campus can be countered through the establishment of a healthy wellbeing culture.

Furthermore, we posit here that a culture that authentically embraces wellbeing and academics' mental wellness can help to drive resources to services that effectively support mental wellbeing but can also encourage academics to access such services, free of the perceived stigma that is so often coupled with mental illness. The establishment of such a culture is by no means a simple task and involves a number of levers to drive a shift in attitudes, practices, perceptions, and behaviours associated with wellness. We conclude by providing various benefits and risks associated with wellbeing services in academia and a call for a more forthright commitment to developing a culture of wellbeing in academia.

We begin by outlining some of the key concerns associated with accessing mental wellbeing support. In particular, what we consider to be accessibility and how the term goes beyond simply physical access. From here we discuss the broader term of 'privacy' and how one's identity must be protected, especially when employment is potentially affected. Finally, we discuss the nuances associated with online support and how this may appear to be a wonderful bridge to create an accessible and private service for all, but also has its own drawbacks.

When Accessibility is Avoided

So, I saw you walking into the psych centre the other day. Does that mean you're crazy?

This was almost word-for-word a statement that was said to one of the authors of this chapter when a colleague saw them walking into an on-campus mental health support service. For many, this experience would have been both confronting and humiliating. Fortunately, the conversation that followed was a very open and honest discussion about mental health in the workplace. Having a healthy and honest discussion about mental health with your work colleagues is not the experience for many who are faced with the stigma of mental illness and the threat of being disadvantaged at work as a result of poor mental wellbeing (Cooper & Barton, 2016; Nelson & Kim, 2011; Stuart, 2006).

This issue highlights that despite an employer having a strong desire to make services available and easily accessible (physically) for employees, this practice does come with drawbacks. Being frank and open about mental wellbeing is not a space some are willing to be in, especially around co-workers and when their liveli-hood may be at risk. As private as a session may be, even being seen to access such services could make a person feel marginalised.

Accessibility options need to move beyond physical location and look more ho-listically at what 'access' means. Access can mean how available services are, how cognitively and emotionally ready academics are to use these services, how stig-matising the service use would be if discovered, or how supportive line managers and the academic administration are of the use of such services. If these access op-tions fail at any point, then even the very best service may be avoided. In particular, the use of in-house services that are funded/controlled by an institution can be seen as a major conflict of interest.

An allied health service (where healthcare workers may be physically present but operate wholly independently and autonomously from the wider organisation) may offer some separation from the felt conflict associated with a centrally controlled service, but the physical closeness does still mean there is the potential for a person to be seen and judged for accessing the service. A wholly separated service that is physically distant and autonomous in nature may appear to be the best option, but this service then becomes less salient and less easy to access physically, meaning time away from the office and a lack of engagement with a service that is not top of mind because it is not physically present on campus. These distanced services also make it seem as though mental wellbeing is not something that is accepted and supported by an institution and should be hidden away on a separate site.

Perhaps having allied health services on campus and at a separate location could be a suitable alternative to balance both these issues, but then the reality of high costs of operation come into being, and where a service is not readily accessed, the institution may feel it is a cost it does not wish to bear. Privacy, for many, becomes a defining factor and has driven some to consider options that are physically and administratively separated from their employer; however, this also has its own is-sues, as we discuss in the next section.

When Privacy is Problematic

The stigma associated with mental wellbeing is clearly problematic (Corrigan & Kleinlein, 2005; Link et al., 1997; Rüsch et al., 2005). The concerns associated with privacy and mental illness have been discussed for decades (c.f. Bates, 1964 as an early work highlighting mental wellbeing's importance) as many societies still consider mental illness to be stigmatised. There are still significant risks to employment if there is a breach of privacy associated with mental illness (Naslund & Aschbrenner, 2019) and any normative acceptance of self-care and wellness is still some way off (Malla et al., 2015; Mizok et al., 2014; Page, 1995), especially in higher education (Gulliver et al., 2019; Quinn et al., 2009). Open discussions regarding mental wellbeing may be becoming more prevalent but they are far from normative enough for many to consider mental illness or poor mental wellbeing to be a safe topic to broach in the workplace.

As such, any behaviours that engage in support seeking activity must be done in a manner that protects the identity of the individual seeking help. It should be noted that even the perception of a conflict can be enough to make a service appear to be inaccessible by those who are deeply concerned about their employer knowing they are seeking mental health support. Again, this comes down to a perpetuated stigma associated with mental illness in the workplace despite the evidence to suggest that is quite prevalent in academia (Block-Lerner & Cardaciotto, 2016), exacerbated by the increasing pressures placed on faculty (Russell & Weigold, 2020).

Chang et al. (2018) studied the role that perceived privacy plays in users' engagement with information disclosure. Their study shows that there are four key factors necessary in order to develop a person's perception of privacy in a given situation: privacy control, privacy risk, privacy concerns, and trust. Their results show that when a person feels they have control over their privacy, they will show a heightened level of perceived privacy in a situation. Control is a powerful tool and one that is often at odds when dealing with mental illness. For example, a sense of being out of control is often associated with anxiety disorders (Hallion et al., 2017), which are commonplace in academia (Eisenberg et al., 2007; Radwan, 2021). As such, enabling a sense of control over one's own privacy and private agenda is central to a sense of perceived privacy in this space *but* is also counter-intuitive to the normalisation of a wellbeing culture that can often involve open and frank conversations regarding wellbeing in the workplace (Sergeant & Laws-Chapman, 2012). In this way, a person may want to feel they are in control of what is and is not disclosed to their employer. All the while, a healthy wellbeing culture would mean there is open disclosure of information, but this information is used as a mechanism to support academics, rather than to use this knowledge against them. This is central to the notion that trust is important in perceived privacy. Where there is an erosion of trust between parties there is also an erosion of perceived privacy. Unfortunately, there is a growing erosion of trust between the academy and administration (Antonowicz et al., 2020; Londono Velez, 2017).

The use of off-site mental wellbeing support services provides a level of physical privacy and perceived control that may not be present in an on-campus service. However, as stated previously, these services also involve time management skills, requests for leave, and potentially after-work appointments that are not conducive to establishing an effective solution or a campus culture that supports wellness. What is also known is that many people experiencing poor mental wellbeing struggle with many of these tasks and the processes involved with making appointments, arranging travel, and ensuring workloads are manageable can become overwhelming and too difficult to overcome for the individual desperately in need of support (Farrer et al., 2016; Ghiasvand et al., 2017; Hoge et al., 2013). Policies to allow for time away from work to access such services may still be avoided if there are monetary costs associated with them. Of course, the academy could provide free services, but this then brings the service provider and the administration into a financial relationship and further exacerbates the perception of a conflict. The perceived lack of privacy can also be a key concern, regardless of how external an off-site provider might be.

One pathway that has been used by a growing number of institutions is online or app based digital wellbeing solutions. Online wellness apps can be always accessed via a digital device with internet connectivity and the margin for human error or accidental disclosure is minimised when the service is wholly automated. The cost for use is relatively low and in a digitally connected world it can feel as though it is a viable solution for our future. However, as with most interventions, online support also has its drawbacks.

When Online is Ineffective

It is always on. It is always available. A digital device can be an excellent way to provide 'nudges' that encourage wellbeing. Despite their obvious advantages, are online tools and wellbeing apps all that effective? There is extensive evidence that shows the use of apps and online tools can provide the ad hoc support and reminder to engage in positive behavioural change (Bakker & Rickard, 2019; Bidargaddi et al., 2017; Finkelstein & Laphsin, 2007; Stallman, 2019). However, what is still to be determined is whether these ad hoc engagements lead to lasting wellness, whether they support the development of a culture of wellbeing, whether they are an effective tool for aiding serious mental wellbeing issues and whether they lead to unintended negative consequences. Veer and Dobele (2021) show that online mental wellbeing apps and online tools can help improve open discussions about mental wellbeing and struggles associated with mental health but can also dissuade some users from seeking professional help. That is, rather than being a supplementary tool that supports other activities online, mental wellbeing tools become a replacement for other services, despite not being as effective. Ideally, a digital device would be used in conjunction with professional medial support but as Veer and Dobele's (2021) research shows, there are always those who feel a digital tool can be supplementary to any other wellbeing support. We also see other online spaces being used to bolster wellness and these places, especially when unmoderated, having a negative impact on wellbeing (Veer & Dobele, 2021).

Ultimately, an online wellness service is only as effective as its proactive and mindful use. Zahrai et al. (2022) show that digital technology can have ongoing negative effects when unconscious use is prevalent, and mindfulness is put to the wayside. There is also the added consequence that a digital device is often connected to multiple external sources at any time and although there may be a heightened perception of perceived privacy, the data being gathered and shared with third-party providers could be extremely exposing to the users. It is unlikely that data about mental wellness app usage would be disclosed to an employer but depending on the app's terms and conditions, the usage may be shared with other parties that use the information to develop a profile of the user for future advertising pressures (Parker et al., 2019).

All in all, the reliance on a digitally connected device requires the conscious and active effort of the participant. Tanouri et al. (2021) have shown that online apps can be beneficial university students' wellbeing when designed effectively, but what is yet to be determined is whether inappropriate or casual use of these online services have a null effect or a determinantal effect on its users. As with all the other services discussed, the use of online apps ultimately needs cognitive capacity, emotional capacity and time allowances to enable them to be effectively utilised. Creating this mindset and culture of self-care and support requires a holistic approach to wellness in the academy. It is important to enable such a culture to promote wellbeing in an authentic manner, as we discuss in the following section.

Enabling a Wellness Culture

Underpinning any service delivery, adoption, and use model in the wellbeing space must be a genuinely authentic approach to creating a culture that promotes safety, belong and care for those struggling with their mental wellbeing. This culture requires an appreciation from all parties that a healthy member of the academy is a more productive member. Utilitarianism aside, a healthy member of an institution is also a happier and more loyal ambassador for their institution. Healthfulness, happiness, loyalty, productivity, and a sense of belonging are all extremely abstract and almost impossible to quantify in any measurable way on a regular basis, but what is evident is that an absence of these constructs creates a culture that is not enjoyable to be a part of and, at worse, can be toxic and harmful.

Te Whare Tapa Whā (A House of Four Walls) is a model of wellbeing drawn from Matāuranga Māori (Māori indigenous knowledge). Te Whare Tapa Whā argues that wellbeing is a function of four equally important factors: physical wellness, emotional wellness, social wellness, and spiritual wellness (Pistacchi, 2008). To place a heavy emphasis on one factor to the detriment of others will result in a drop in wellbeing. This is not a model that is solely used in indigenous contexts but is a model of wellbeing adopted in a number of larger organisations in New Zealand to embrace wellbeing as an holistic approach rather than focusing on a single factor or, indeed, being wholly responsive to a drop in wellness (Chand, 2020; Hazou et al., 2021). An authentic approach to developing a wellbeing culture would be to proactively create and maintain a culture that embraces wellbeing as being as important as work productivity. This means embracing all aspects of wellness beyond the physical and mental but crucially the social, too. Does a person in the academy feel part of a collective and feel they have the supporters around them to make effective choices about self-care and personal wellbeing? If not, then this aspect of wellbeing should be addressed.

Similarly, Barton and Grant's (2006) health map puts people and community as being central to the health and wellbeing of a wider system. Without a focus on individuals and the community, the possibility of developing a proactive and efficacious wellbeing system is limited, regardless of how effective the provided

On-site support

Full Separation and Autonomous

May be seen by peers using services, adding to the stigma

Stigma and perceived risk to employment

Institution Controlled

Feels hidden rather than embraced

Harder to physically access

Off-site support

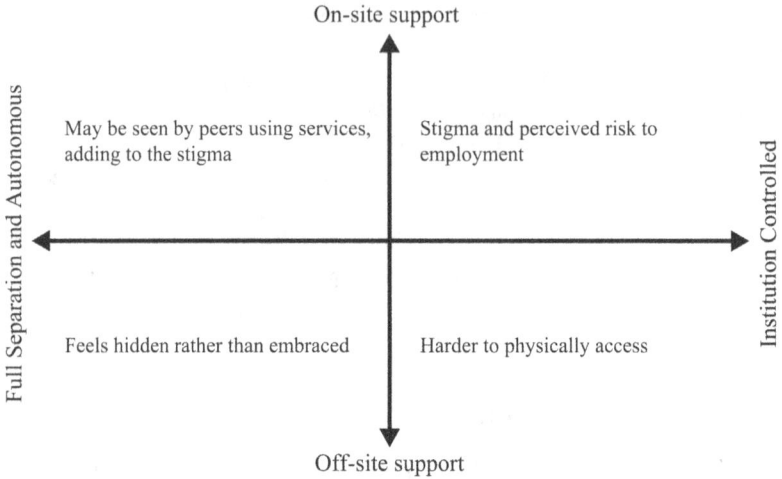

Figure 3.1 Impact of Wellbeing Services On- and Off-Campus

services are. This systemic approach to understanding wellbeing interventions is neither easy nor cheap (Veer et al., 2020) but it is, in our reasoning, essential to promote access to wellbeing services irrespective of their location.

Figure 3.1 shows some of the negatives of wellbeing support services where no culture of acceptance is present. This diagrammatic representation focuses more on what the issues may be but also where a culture of wellbeing may provide answers. That is, if an institution is not seeing an uptake in on-campus autonomous services, how can this be overcome and what can be done to combat this lack of uptake? Building a sense of perceived privacy and control may help, but also building a greater sense of support and collective wellbeing in the campus culture will mean even if someone is seen accessing these services they are not vilified for their focus on self-care. This is the power that a wellbeing culture brings. In effect, access to services may be present but also avoided unless there is a culture of acceptance and willingness to support mental wellbeing by the institution, even at a cost.

The Relative Costs and Benefits of Wellbeing Services

It is our contention that any service offering, in any form will be fraught until a culture of wellness and support is normalised within an institution and, potentially, in our society. This is not to say that offerings should not be enabled and provided immediately to start to support academics in their wellbeing journey. Table 3.1 outlines the various offerings discussed in this chapter and summarises some of the concerns outlined and benefits that could be gained from their implementation for both users of the services and the wider institution.

Table 3.1 Summary of Risks and Benefits of Different Wellbeing Intervention Models

Service		Users	Institutions	Impact on Wellbeing Culture
Verified online, app-based mental wellbeing support	Benefits	• Anonymity can help to improve perceived control and perceived privacy • Easily accessible • Good apps can show evidence of impact and improvement • Requires little time off • Relatively cheap to access, even if paid for personally • Regular reminders can mean wellbeing and self-care is normalised into a person's daily routine	• Signals a commitment to wellbeing in a proactive sense and not just as a reactive measure when wellbeing is poor • Measurable usage by staff • Can be relatively cheap to implement	• Likely to be low, at best, but a mass approach to wellbeing could help to normalise self-care and other help services • Could give the impression that staff need to 'help themselves' rather than be supported by the institution • Token approach to wellness • Best offerings are integrated with other services so that users can access additional options beyond the app itself, to help show a concerted and systemic commitment to wellbeing culture
	Risks	• Rarely personalised • Sometimes not effective at supporting significant mental illness issues • May be used as supplementary to professional care • Low likelihood of long-term uptake unless personal commitment is evident • Low social focus and so users are usually isolated even further in their wellbeing journey • Without monitoring the online forums, some apps can be harmful	• Can be accused of doing the bare minimum • Could deter use of other professional health support • Could be seen as a tokenistic approach to wellbeing, rather than a real commitment to it • Can deter open conversations about wellbeing as focus is pushed to online spaces	

(Continued)

Table 3.1 (Continued)

Service		Users	Institutions	Impact on Wellbeing Culture
On-campus wellbeing support services operated by the institution	Benefits	• Services are easily accessible, physically • Services can be developed and tailored for the needs of those accessing them • Offer a sense of support from one's institution and value	• Seen as supportive of staff wellbeing • Purposive focus on the specific needs that face their culture and strategy	• Can demonstrate a level of support from the institution that profits are set aside for the wellbeing of staff • Can normalise a wellbeing culture by being physically present and tailored for academic staff, rather than relying on outsourced services
	Risks	• The closeness to the institution can impact a sense of privacy and the alignment with the institution could be perceived as a lack of control, especially when trust in administrators is low	• Can be costly and require additional administrative structures to effectively create, manage and monitor the services • Can have unintended consequences of high use that is not legitimate, compromising productivity	• Costly and potentially easily cut when efficacy/uptake is not effectively demonstrated

(Continued)

Table 3.1 (Continued)

Service		Users	Institutions	Impact on Wellbeing Culture
On campus, third-party wellbeing services	Benefits	• A separation from the administration helps to add a heightened sense of control and agency • Easily accessible and likely to be perceived as being of better quality as it is run by professionals/experts rather than created by the university itself	• Easy access for staff and shows a commitment to using professionals • Signals a commitment to wellness and can help normalise self-care as part of the culture with it being visible on campus • Likely easier and cheaper to manage given that a third-party will be taking much of the control • Could still get reports from the third-party operator on use and engagement • Easier to disestablish if uptake is not strong	• Often seen as the best model as it blends the expertise of a third-party operator with the cost savings that come from not needing to manage the operation • Unless it is well advertised, supported and encouraged the services could go under-utilised and be a heavy cost to bear • A third-party operator may not signal as strong a commitment to wellbeing, especially if they are asked to regularly justify their presence on campus
	Risks	• lack of physical privacy involved • May still require time away from work to access the services • If oversubscribed the wait associated with seeking help could be unwieldy	• Physical space needs on campus means other 'core' services cannot be operated there • Can be costly to have services on campus and paid to a third-party supplier with little	

(Continued)

Table 3.1 (Continued)

Service		Users	Institutions	Impact on Wellbeing Culture
Off-campus, third-party wellbeing services	Benefits	• Separated entirely from the institution to enable heightened perceived privacy and control • May be greater offerings for	• Physical separation means a university does not need to support on-campus space for wellbeing services, which can be often at a premium • Perceived separation can help to encourage those who do not trust the institution • Likely to have the lowest cost to the institution • Many providers available meaning options available to choose from	• Not a great advertisement for wellbeing culture by seemingly pushing it off-site • Availability may be better than nothing but without a presence on campus it may feel as though this is an afterthought • Can be very easily disestablished and risk to ongoing commitment is high
	Risks	• May require additional time management organisation • May require time away from campus or after work, adding a burden to self-care • Services may not be specifically tailored to the nuanced nature of academia and more generic in approach	• May see more time away from campus by staff using the services • Less control over how the services are used means inappropriate access may be exploited by some • Service providers may not understand the academic context well and efficacy of support may not be suitable for staff	

As with anything, the cost of operation will vary by institution and demand as well as the efficacy will be determined by the quality of service on offer. Some may be better than others and some will be better aligned, culturally, to the needs of the academic community being served. There would also need to be careful consideration of the nuanced power dynamics at play within an academic institution. How will services be made available to academic staff and how does that differ across seniority levels? How will the culture of an institution respond to the knowledge that a senior professor with high leadership responsibilities is seeking wellbeing support? In a healthy, welcoming wellbeing culture this would be equally encouraged, but in a competitive and toxic culture this knowledge may impact their perceived ability to lead others. The development and implementation efficacy of these services need to be carefully considered but are not the focus of this chapter.

Concluding Remarks

If there was an easy solution, every institution would implement it. We are in a place where mental wellbeing is seen as vital for academic staff but how this is supported remains in its infancy. Successful interventions to support specific individuals or groups may exist. However, without a commitment by the academy to a whole of system culture of wellbeing any services made available, whether on or off-campus or online, or combinations of offerings, are likely to be met with resistance and scepticism, especially when trust in leadership is low. Once again, a culture of wellbeing must be front and centre in order for any academic wellbeing initiative to be effective. If the services being put in place affect culture negatively, then this should be seriously considered above the cost to implement such a service. Similarly, if it means an improvement in culture then this should be factored into a business case to show how a university culture that values its staff can offer additional productivity, support, and wellness for years to come. Ultimately, it is on those in power to determine the priorities of wellbeing and whether the wellness of its staff is important enough to fiscally support services that promote a positive wellbeing culture and intervene when wellbeing is low. Individual champions can lead initiatives and dive grassroots change; however, these are often the same very caring, very well meaning, very diligent academics and professional staff who take on additional work to benefit those around them. To tax these individuals because they care is a pathway to their own exhaustion and burnout. As such, it may be everyone's duty to create a culture of wellness, but unless it is led by those in leadership, we believe it is unlikely to be systemically adopted throughout the institution.

Reflection by Ekant Veer (First Author)

There is a romanticism about being an academic that perhaps filled me as a naïve 20-something year old who returned to university to pursue an academic career. On reflection, I appreciate that no workplace is perfect but when you see systems, structures, practices, expectations, and culture all colluding to make life tough (and for some, inequitably tougher), it wipes the sheen away from a career that should be a privilege.

I am emboldened by the constant strive for greater wellbeing services and what appears to be a deep desire by administrators to truly provide support for staff, but until expectations, workload, and pressure are addressed, no service is going to make massive difference. The systems, structures, policies and culture need to shift if we're to truly see support services utilised and wellbeing put to the forefront of our institutions' minds. Until then, we'll see some succeed and others fall by the wayside. We'll justify why some never made it in a way that makes it easier to cope, but eventually we will need to accept that as a field we are not supporting everyone who needs us. We are not doing enough, and, in time, we will either continue to ignore that fact and cope the best we can, or we'll start to see institutions shift and revolutionise wellbeing culture.

I've tried to reflect this goal in the reflective image, shown in Figure 3.2. I propose that all elements (culture, systems, policies, staff, students, and the broader community) must work together to achieve a wellbeing culture. However, without people in between them, bringing the different elements together, they may operate in isolation, rather than in collaboration to promote wellbeing.

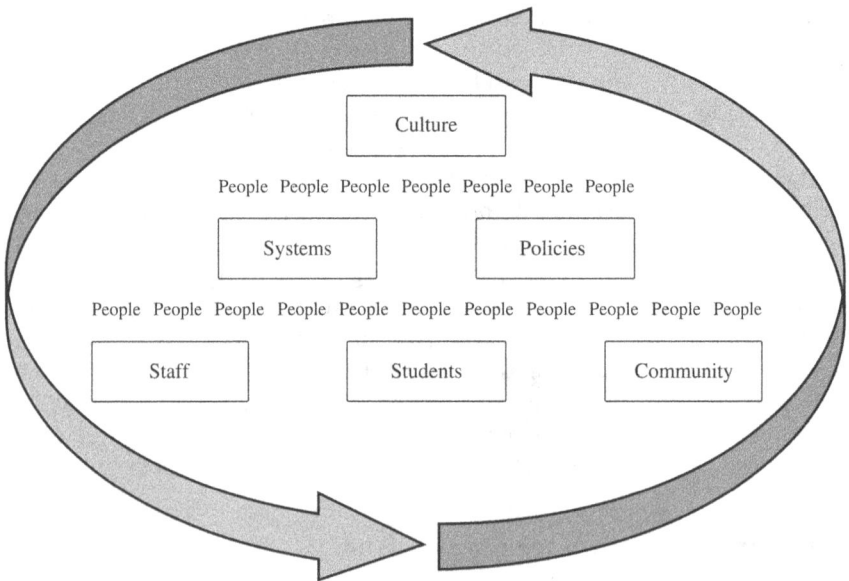

Figure 3.2 Reflection Drawing – A Holistic Approach to Building a Wellbeing Culture

References

Abery, E., & Gunson, J. S. (n.d). The cycle of student and staff wellbeing: Emotional labour and extension requests in higher education. *A Practice Report. Student Success, 7*(1), 65–71.

Antonowicz, D., Kulczycki, E., & Budzanowska, A. (2020). Breaking the deadlock of mistrust? A participative model of the structural reforms in higher education in Poland. *Higher Education Quarterly, 74*(4), 391–409.

Bakker, D., & Rickard, N. (2019). Engagement with a cognitive behavioural therapy mobile phone app predicts changes in mental health and wellbeing: MoodMission. *Australian Psychologist, 54*(4), 245–260.

Barton, H., & Grant, M. (2006). A health map for the local human habitat. *The Journal of the Royal Society for the Promotion of Health, 126*(6), 252–253.

Bates, A. P. (1964). Privacy—A useful concept. *Social Forces, 42*(4), 429–434.

Bidargaddi, N., Musiat, P., Winsall, M., Vogl, G., Blake, V., Quinn, S., Orlowski, S., Antezana, G., & Schrader, G. (2017). Efficacy of a web-based guided recommendation service for a curated list of readily available mental health and well-being Mobile apps for young people: Randomized controlled trial. *Journal of Medical Internet Research, 19*(5), e6775.

Block-Lerner, J., & Cardaciotto, L. (2016). *The mindfulness-informed educator*. Routledge.

Bromley, R. (2006). On and off campus: Colleges and universities as local stakeholders. *Planning Practice and Research, 21*(1), 1–24.

Chand, B. S.-K. (2020). Improving teaching practice through indigenous learning models. *Te Kaharoa, 13*(1), Article 1.

Chang, Y., Wong, S. F., Libaque-Saenz, C. F., & Lee, H. (2018). The role of privacy policy on consumers' perceived privacy. *Government Information Quarterly, 35*(3), 445–459.

Cooper, K., & Barton, G. C. (2016). An exploration of physical activity and wellbeing in university employees. *Perspectives in Public Health, 136*(3), 152–160.

Corrigan, P. W., & Kleinlein, P. (2005). The impact of mental illness stigma. In P. W. Corrigan (Ed.), *On the stigma of mental illness: Practical strategies for research and social change* (pp. 11–44). American Psychological Association.

Eisenberg, D., Gollust, S. E., Golberstein, E., & Hefner, J. L. (2007). Prevalence and correlates of depression, anxiety, and suicidality among university students. *American Journal of Orthopsychiatry, 77*(4), 534–542.

Essential elements of organizational initiatives to improve workplace wellbeing. (2017). In *The routledge companion to wellbeing at work* (pp. 314–331). Routledge.

Farrer, L. M., Gulliver, A., Bennett, K., Fassnacht, D. B., & Griffiths, K. M. (2016). Demographic and psychosocial predictors of major depression and generalised anxiety disorder in Australian university students. *BMC Psychiatry, 16*(1), 241.

Finkelstein, J., & Laphsin, O. (2007). Reducing depression stigma using a web-based program. *International Journal of Medical Informatics, 76*(10), 726–734.

Ghiasvand, A. M., Naderi, M., Tafreshi, M. Z., Ahmadi, F., & Hosseini, M. (2017). Relationship between time management skills and anxiety and academic motivation of nursing students in Tehran. *Electronic Physician, 9*(1), 3678–3684.

Gulliver, A., Farrer, L., Bennett, K., & Griffiths, K. M. (2019). University staff mental health literacy, stigma and their experience of students with mental health problems. *Journal of Further and Higher Education, 43*(3), 434–442.

Hallion, L. S., Tolin, D. F., Assaf, M., Goethe, J., & Diefenbach, G. J. (2017). Cognitive control in generalized anxiety disorder: Relation of inhibition impairments to worry and anxiety severity. *Cognitive Therapy and Research, 41*(4), 610–618.

Hazou, R., Woodland, S., & Ilgenfritz, P. (2021). Performing te whare Tapa whā: Building on cultural rights to decolonise prison theatre practice. *Research in Drama Education: The Journal of Applied Theatre and Performance, 26*(3), 494–510.

Hoge, E. A., Bui, E., Marques, L., Metcalf, C. A., Morris, L. K., Robinaugh, D. J., Worthington, J. J., Pollack, M. H., & Simon, N. M. (2013). Randomized controlled trial of mindfulness meditation for generalized anxiety disorder: Effects on anxiety and stress reactivity. *The Journal of Clinical Psychiatry, 74*(8), 16662.

Lashuel, H. A. (2020). What about faculty? *ELife, 9*, e54551.

Link, B. G., Struening, E. L., Rahav, M., Phelan, J. C., & Nuttbrock, L. (1997). On stigma and its consequences: Evidence from a longitudinal study of men with dual diagnoses of mental illness and substance abuse. *Journal of Health and Social Behavior, 38*(2), 177–190.

Londono Velez, A. F. (2017). The Trust/Mistrust tension between the academy and the management at university. *Ágora U.S.B, 17*(1), 281–287.

Malla, A., Joober, R., & Garcia, A. (2015). "Mental illness is like any other medical illness": A critical examination of the statement and its impact on patient care and society. *Journal of Psychiatry and Neuroscience: JPN, 40*(3), 147–150.

Mizok, L., Russinova, Z., & Millner, U. C. (2014). Acceptance of mental illness: Core components of a multifaceted construct. *Psychological Services, 11*(1), 97–104.

Mudrak, J., Zabrodska, K., Kveton, P., Jelinek, M., Blatny, M., Solcova, I., & Machovcova, K. (2018). Occupational well-being among university faculty: A job demands-resources model. *Research in Higher Education, 59*(3), 325–348.

Naslund, J. A., & Aschbrenner, K. A. (2019). Risks to privacy with use of social media: Understanding the views of social media users with serious mental illness. *Psychiatric Services, 70*(7), 561–568.

Nelson, R. E., & Kim, J. (2011). The impact of mental illness on the risk of employment termination. *The Journal of Mental Health Policy and Economics, 14*(1), 39–52.

O'Brien, T., & Guiney, D. (2018). Staff Wellbeing in Higher Education: A research study for Education Support Partnership. Education Support Partnership. https://healthyuniversities.ac.uk/wp-content/uploads/2019/05/staff_wellbeing_he_research.pdf

Page, S. (1995). Effects of the mental illness label in 1993. *Journal of Health and Social Policy, 7*(2), 61–68.

Parker, L., Halter, V., Karliychuk, T., & Grundy, Q. (2019). How private is your mental health app data? An empirical study of mental health app privacy policies and practices. *International Journal of Law and Psychiatry, 64*, 198–204.

Pistacchi, A. (2008). Te whare Tapa wha: The four cornerstones of maori health and patricia Grace's dogside story. *Journal of New Zealand Literature: JNZL, 26*, 136–152.

Quinn, N., Wilson, A., MacIntyre, G., & Tinklin, T. (2009). 'People look at you differently': Students' experience of mental health support within higher education. *British Journal of Guidance and Counselling, 37*(4), 405–418.

Radwan, A. S. (2021). Anxiety among university staff during Covid-19 pandemic: A cross-sectional study. *Journal of Nursing and Health Science, 10*(2), 1–8.

Roos, B. H., & Borkoski, C. C. (2021). Attending to the teacher in the teaching: Prioritizing faculty well-being. *Perspectives of the ASHA Special Interest Groups, 6*(4), 831–840.

Rüsch, N., Angermeyer, M. C., & Corrigan, P. W. (2005). Mental illness stigma: Concepts, consequences, and initiatives to reduce stigma. *European Psychiatry, 20*(8), 529–539.

Russell, E. J., & Weigold, I. K. (2020). Work stress and comfort in university faculty: Do gender and academic field matter? *Journal of Employment Counseling, 57*(3), 130–142.

Sergeant, J., & Laws-Chapman, C. (2012). Creating a positive workplace culture. *Nursing Management, 18*(9), 14–19.

Spence, G. (2015). Workplace wellbeing programs: If you build it they may NOT come… because it's not what they really need. *International Journal of Wellbeing, 5*(2), Article 2.

Stallman, H. M. (2019). Efficacy of the my coping plan Mobile application in reducing distress: A randomised controlled trial. *Clinical Psychologist, 23*(3), 206–212.

Stuart, H. (2006). Mental illness and employment discrimination. *Current Opinion in Psychiatry, 19*(5), 522–526.

Stuckey, S. M., Collins, B. T., Patrick, S., Grove, K. S., & Ward, E. (2019). Thriving vs surviving: Benefits of formal mentoring program on faculty well-being. *International Journal of Mentoring and Coaching in Education, 8*(4), 378–396.

Taggart, G. (2021). Administrative intensity and faculty job stress. *Innovative Higher Education, 46*(5), 605–621.

Tanouri, A., Kennedy, A.-M., & Veer, E. (2021). A conceptual framework for transformative gamification services. *Journal of Services Marketing, 36*(2), 185–200.

Veer, E., & Dobele, A. (2021). Big boys don't cry [offline]: The phygital disconnect between online and offline mental wellness engagement. *Journal of Strategic Marketing*, 1–21. https://doi.org/10.1080/0965254X.2021.1965190

Veer, E., Golf-Papez, M., & Zahrai, K. (2020). Using the socio-ecological model as an holistic approach to behavioural change. In A. M. Kennedy (Ed.), *Macro-social marketing insights: Systems thinking for wicked problems* (p. 25). Routledge.

Zahrai, K., Veer, E., Ballantine, P. W., de Vries, H. P., & Prayag, G. (2022). Either you control social media or social media controls you: Understanding the impact of self-control on excessive social media use from the dual-system perspective. *Journal of Consumer Affairs, 56*(2), 806–848.

Part II

Introduction to Part II

Wellbeing at the Individual Level

Angela R. Dobele and Lisa Farrell

Introduction

This part of the resource explores individual wellbeing considerations including identity and practice. In the first chapter in this section, Chapter 4, Meg Elkins reflects on the negotiation of our academic selves within the context of the higher education institutions and departments to which we belong. In Chapter 5, Kate Hynes offers an international perspective as she reflects on her self-introduced wellbeing strategies as part of negotiating balance between work and life, and a wellbeing mindset. And our final chapter in this section, Jonathan Boymal, Sam Sterling, Craig Williamson, Ying Zhou and Patrick Lynch, consider the factors that individuals in academia can influence in defence of their own wellbeing and offer discussion around the policies, practices and approaches that impact us and our colleagues every day.

The increasing prevalence and severity of wellbeing-related issues in higher education is a critical issue and individually lead approaches are an important part of the needed attention. Afterall, if we, staff at the grassroots, cannot or will not lead this revolution, who will? All three chapters offer practical considerations for individuals seeking to implement wellbeing practice or refine or adapt existing approaches.

DOI: 10.4324/9781003284772-6

Chapter 4

Academic Identities and Wellbeing Practices

Meg Elkins

Introduction

We are all part of something – whether we like it or not. In life, we find tribes that we identify with. In academia, these tribes can be assigned or ascribed through others, for example, at the university to which an individual belongs, by discipline, by managerial hierarchies or through identities that resonate with an individual, be it gender, ethnicity, age or ability. These groups can be based on individuals' physical, social or mental characteristics. Social identity describes how one's own (and others' perception of one's) group belonging can cause intergroup effects, creating favourable treatment of in-group members relative to out-group members (Tajfel & Turner, 1979). Tajfel (1978) was the first seminal study that introduced the term social identity theory to explain how groups and group memberships impact an individual's self-perception of how to behave. Identity is part of human nature.

Identity

When humans meet others, several behavioural shortcuts are used to categorise whether or not that individual can be trusted. These shortcuts are known as heuristics and make it easier to navigate decision-making or create "rules of thumb" as we can process up to 35,000 decisions daily (Sahakian & LaBuzetta, 2013). When meeting new people, individuals often go through this process: Is the face someone we recognise? Could that person be a threat? Or is that person like us or not? The last question here is critical: How do primal human brains understand threats? It is part of a human survival mechanism. So, these heuristics are looking for a sense that the other individual is similar to us in some way, discipline, work experience, background or interests – once this is established, it reduces the threat. We can relax and find an ally.

Organisational Identity

Identity adds another layer to navigating "who has our backs". Organisational Identity, outlined initially by Albert et al. (1985), argued that an organisation's

DOI: 10.4324/9781003284772-7

identity was constituted by a set of claims regarding what was central, distinctive, and enduring. In the higher education system, the role of the organisational identity falls around the roles it is designed to perform. For academics, there are three specific values: (i) research, (ii) teaching, and (iii) service and administration. For many, academic success is built on being research active (Haynes & Fearfull, 2008). However, the identity of a faculty member is also built on other roles, such as teaching, engagement, and administration. Research active involves connecting to your discipline and being recognised for your work in that community of practice to get published and funding through grants. Much of this consists in being able to network and collaborate. Herein lies the role of social identity and a sense of belonging. To succeed in academia, you must be able to imbue the characteristics of the university's organisational identity, your discipline's social identity, and your values, to forge a path. Many disaffected academics lament the difficulty of breaking into the club or playing the "rules of the game". The challenge in academia is to be part of the in-group that will support your values and career ambitions.

This chapter explores how social identity impacts the academic workplace. It examines how we can develop conscious competencies around our social identities. It also goes back to the root of in-groups and out-groups, as discussed by researchers in the 1970s and 1980s. The chapter explores the role of reciprocity in groups and how this behaviour can help generate an authentic self-identity at work, which can become part of your narrative. The next section examines how conflict can arise when the individual's values and beliefs clash with the organisation's values, with some tips on how to navigate this conflict. The final section gives some tips on how to move towards a group-oriented leader.

Base Social Identity

Your social identities, both the ones you claim and those ascribed to you, change from context to context. It may influence how you create your professional life: The ideas you come up with, the assumptions and constraints you are working with, and even the structural barriers you are contending with. Sociologist Pierre Bourdieu (1980) proposes this is a form of reflexive sociology whereby one can recognise the biases and assumptions as a form of sensemaking; he states that understanding these identities as sources of power can explain social asymmetries and hierarchies, which can help social emancipation.

Generally, social identities can fall under the following categories: ability status, gender, ethnicity, academic discipline, national origin/citizenship, race, political identity, sexual orientation attraction and other characteristics. Some groups can be oppressed and marginalised, which may mean that there is not equal access to resources in the university system. Equally, some groups hold earned or unearned privileges in institutions, meaning they have greater access to resources that can shape culture at an institutional level.

By an individual understanding these elements, one can see how it:

- Can impact how you see yourself as a person.
- Can impact your awareness as to how frequently these issues are in your thoughts.
- Can impact your views and values and how you relate to work.
- Can impact your views and values and how you live your life.
- Informs who you collaborate with and who you spend your time with.
- Can allow us to understand how these can change over time.

Part of identifying which groups individuals feel like they belong to or assign themselves can add contexts to help individuals define themselves. Understanding these elements can help navigate an academic develop conscious competencies. It can also help to know where one might want to get to.

Within academic groups, it is important to understand how an individual learns to develop skills and effective habits that influence their professional choices. Maslow's (1943) four stages of learning unpack how we go from being unaware to having developed skilled or effective habits.

Bringing awareness to this helps deepen your conscious competency and your performance as a professional, beginning with issues arising from the lack of awareness at the first stage of our careers. For example, completing a PhD and transitioning into an academic position, unaware of the expectations of academic responsibilities.

In this first stage, you are unaware that you are unaware. In the second stage, you are aware you have gaps in your skill level to be competent; perhaps you need to develop a research track record but lack awareness of how to bridge this gap. An understanding that you have gaps can explain the third stage, conscious incompetence. The penultimate stage is slightly clumsy as we use a step-by-step approach to navigate conscious competency. At this stage, you are developing the skills of creating a research track record, but it is not natural; there is uncertainty about the best approach to completer tasks. The final element of unconscious competency is in the skilled stage, where one is not second-guessing how to react and respond. Here the academic has developed mastery of research skills and is part of the in-group with full awareness of what is required to be an academic with a tenure track. With social identity, it takes time to become part of a group. There are stages of learning to integrate the social norms and behaviour of the group you would like to belong to. To move beyond the awareness stage and apply your knowledge to create a skilled professional identity adeptly requires awareness, much like the process one goes through learning how to drive a car.

In-Group and Out-Group Bias

How do we find people in our "in-group"? Once we see someone as part of our in-group, we can move out of defensive mode to be more charming – we are more likely to feel empathy or celebrate their successes (Webb, 2017). We treat our in-group to some degree like versions of ourselves. Not surprisingly, recruitment specialists are more likely to hire based on traits similar to themselves – not on any deep assessments but more on similar attributes and interests.

This hiring practice can be subject to what is known as unconscious bias. Evidence of this in academia was revealed in an experiment by Milkman et al. (2015), where potential doctoral students emailed to request a 10-minute meeting with PhD supervisors. The students' names varied: some were male and female, and each sounded white, African American, Chinese, Indian, or Hispanic. While the response rate to an interview was 70 per cent, faculty were more likely to respond to white male requests than those who were not white male (even if this was not their demographic). Bohnet (2016) suggests that the process of de-biasing is difficult. We have an in-built default to use group characteristics when judging other people. To overcome default bias, there needs to be movement beyond awareness training to make people within a system take on more reasoned judgement strategies, such as considering the opposite.

If we have an in-group, we must also describe an out-group. Here is where discrimination emerges. Those in the in-group become the "us", and those in the out-group become "them". The "us" and "them" mentality can be the basis for what Henri Tajfel in the 1970s discovered in his seminal paper "Experiments in Intergroup Discrimination". Tajfel found that discrimination varies in its targets and intensity across cultures. We treat the out-group with degrees of suspicion. They have two dimensions: People treat others in their group better (in-group favouritism) than those of other groups (out-group rejection).

Individuals from such social identity groups often manage social identity to reduce these negative experiences (Goffman, 1963). This process of social identity management can include attempts to suppress or conceal identity and decisions to openly manifest or reveal that identity (Clair et al., 2005). This identity crafting can be seen by the social media persona and images that academics craft on professional platforms such as LinkedIn or Twitter. This crafting can be further managed through the narrative, and social media posts demonstrate who they are and what they represent.

One important concept in understanding social identity is the concept of the minimal group paradigm. Tajfel et al. (1971) developed an experimental paradigm called the minimal group paradigm, whereby any explanation of intergroup discrimination in terms of prejudice, conflict or stereotypes could be ruled out. The results of this research led to the formulation of social identity theory (Tajfel & Turner, 1979). Even if membership is a perceived similarity of a group possessing an arbitrary skill – it shows in-group bias. Some of the early experiments allocated groups through something as random as a coin flip can still create in-group bias. (Diehl, 1990; Jetten et al., 1996; Tajfel et al., 1971)

Group membership determines shared identity and, therefore, a sense of self. With social identity, people pursue their own groups' interests despite no apparent benefit to themselves. A shared understanding of us can affect our attention, perception, memory, and emotions. Insignificant differences can create a divide. When people categorise themselves as part of a group, their self-concept shifts from the individual to the collective level, a process termed social identification. Categorising oneself as a group member significantly influences basic intergroup perception, evaluation, and behaviours seen (Van Bavel & Cunningham, 2009).

Reciprocity and Bias

Biases and heuristics can significantly affect how individuals perceive and interact with social identities. While group identities take hold, they can also trigger bias. Here is the difficulty as we work for organisations and institutions that can go against our personal values. So, identifying with a group can create what I see as reciprocal arrangements to help those we see as "like us".

Reciprocal disclosure means that we need to be able to give a little to get what we need. (Sprecher et al., 2013). Within an organisation, reciprocity can help define who will support us and who we can give support to when we need it.

In behavioural economics, bias explains a tendency to favour a particular group or individuals based on preconceived notions, stereotypes, and prejudices. These group memberships can be based on gender, race, nationality, religion, or other shared characteristics. To be clear, we can identify with many groups, but often we assign a ranking to these groups. For example, in academia, a bias towards a certain methodology that defines your discipline (i.e., quantitative methods over qualitative methods), as does the ability to publish in top-tier journals, could lead you to perceive your group as superior to others. However, other biases can also result in discriminatory behaviour.

The heuristics that allow us to make quick and efficient decisions can also impact how we interact with others. Often in life, we make good but not great decisions. An example of this is the way certain biases impact our decision-making. Take a well-known bias, confirmation bias, whereby individuals seek out information that confirms their beliefs and attitudes, which means that cognitive dissonance may discount or ignore information that does not endorse or reinforce this view. This bias can lead to discrimination and reinforced stereotypes, which may mean we can overestimate or underestimate the likelihood of events and, therefore, don't make the best decisions.

We can also use a heuristic called representativeness which can impact the status quo bias. Based on anecdotal evidence, some people may believe they are not representative of a typical academic in that discipline, which may mean that they discount the possibility of entering that discipline – this is often the case with women in STEM. Here people tend to stick to the status quo of what they know and understand. Therefore, breaking through these barriers in academia means checking unconscious bias of who is or is not included in our groups, faculties, and organisations.

Carolyn Webb's (2017) book "How to Have a Good Day at Work" draws on behavioural science research to overcome feeling like an outsider within a group and connect with others around you. Here are her four tips for creating a sense of belonging:

1 Find a shared interest – within academia, this could be as much as shared interests in topics, methodologies, and preferences in ways of working. However, on a personal level, it could be music, hobbies, clothing or leisure activities.
2 Find a common goal – within academia, this could be finding a research project that resonates with your team that you can work on together. Find out what matters to you most and identify ways to achieve a common goal.
3 Talk about a common vent – most academic staff have excellent levels of critical analysis so it will not be surprising that there are common complaints that are relevant at most universities. Allow others to find a complaint and make sure it is not overly personal or critical.

Echoing the person's words back makes them feel heard and validated. Most academics choose this profession because they believe their work contributes to meaningful outcomes. According to the job characteristic theory receiving feedback and knowing that your work is more than just a cog in the wheel is one of the most powerful ways to keep an employee motivated. In the workplace, whom we identify with has ramifications for how we behave and how that behaviour impacts our relationships with those around us. Whom you identify with indicates whom you would like to imitate. In the current digital environment, the workplace can also extend to whom you follow and identify with on professional social media sites such as LinkedIn or Twitter.

In an academic workplace – narrative is essential. To get a promotion, one must identify and exemplify the organisational values. In the academic context, the alignment between the organisational identity and the individual's social identity helps an individual feel a sense of wellbeing and belonging. When these are out of alignment, this can create a personal internal conflict.

Identity Conflict

When one struggles with an internal conflict at work, one often struggles between being authentic to oneself and one's values. According to Shalom Schwartz et al. (2012), values are used to characterise cultural groups, societies, and individuals, to trace change over time, and to explain the motivational bases of attitudes and behaviour. Values can be cultural and personal. Researchers find attitudes are specific to particular objects and momentary, whereas values are more enduring, higher-level, general evaluations (Rokeach, 1973). There are seven personal value principles outlined by Schwartz et al. (2012). These become rules of thumb that we navigate in our lives. These values, such as professionalism or integrity, are also applied in academic circumstances here. Work value researchers have assumed that a limited number of broad orientations towards work underlie people's ideas of what is important to them when making occupational choices. Values are beliefs linked inextricably to affect. When values are activated, they become infused with feeling. Here, values elicit emotion; that is:

- Values refer to desirable goals that motivate action.
- Values transcend specific actions and situations. This distinguishes values from norms and attitudes that usually refer to specific actions, objects, or situations.
- Values serve as standards or criteria. Values enter awareness when the actions or judgments one considers have conflicting implications for the values one cherishes. This is particularly relevant when evaluating actions, people or events.
- Values are ordered by importance relative to one another. People's values form an ordered system of priorities that characterise them as individuals.
- The relative importance of multiple values guides how one acts. The trade-off among relevant, competing values guides attitudes and behaviours.
- Values consciously or unconsciously motivate behaviour, perceptions, and attitudes.

These personal values determine an organisational-individual fit. Organisational identity is a concept that can highlight important values and norms of the university in an era where most positive connotations of the traditional labels characterising them have been lost. Organisational identity is a concept that can be used to analyse universities as institutions at a time when strong forces are seeking to transform them into organisations. Schwartz (2014) used the individual-level values data to derive a system of seven value dimensions that characterise cultures (i.e., culture at the level of the group). These capture the value emphases that societies set to regulate behaviour and address their basic survival.

Academic work in higher education has been re-shaped, and the university sector changes have become consumer-driven (Harris, 2005) and increasingly bureaucratised (Debowski, 2007). In a shift to address economic priorities, there has been increased competition with other higher education institutions to attract more fee-paying students. Marginson (2000) refers to the danger of research being policy-led, and research identities being colonised as a result of the new research economy. As the roles of an academic change with more and more roles that an academic is expected to fulfil, overload and conflict create tension for wellbeing and job performance. Among these higher expectations, knowing who you are and what your role is, are crucial to know what, as an academic, you say "yes" to and what you say "no" to. Having a clear personal narrative will give a great sense of purpose to help when asked to take on additional research projects, teaching loads, and administrative tasks.

Authentic Whole Self at Work

Authenticity has a ring to it that you know when you see. It is defined as the degree to which an individual's thoughts, feelings, and behaviours are consistent with their inner self, values, and beliefs. In psychology, this is represented by how a person is true to their personality or character, despite the pressure of social norms (Wood et al., 2008). In sociology, this is about "being oneself" in a world of conformity (Erickson, 1995). In philosophy, it's the idea of self-knowledge and self-realisation. Here it relates to ethical and moral ideals to live a meaningful life. Heidegger et al. (1962) suggests that one is neither authentic or inauthentic but more or less so. When one is authentic, we feel aligned and live our values. However, the challenge to turn up and align to our core values is tested in conflict.

An authentic relationship creates reciprocal effects with an inclusive, ethical, caring, and strength-based organisational climate. Reciprocity is key here, as is feeling valued and appreciated by your leadership by your peers. Then individuals can connect their sense of belonging alongside self-identification; it defines who and what they are.

There are layers in an organisation's identity and points where the individual can be subordinate to the organisation, navigating how you can find your place in these institutions. The dual identity model (Dovidio et al., 1998) suggests that making both superordinate and subordinate identities simultaneously salient may enhance cooperation. The superordinate identity is seen as the entire organisation, while the subordinate identity is seen as individual groups. According to Marginson (2007), the university's mission and identity combine enabling conditions that answer the question about institutional specialisation and strategy. Specialisation, in essence, is constituted by one or another mix and quality of products – teaching, research, scholarship, and knowledge transfer.

For academics, keeping this mission salient reminds employees they all share a common interest in the organisation's success and that working together will benefit all. But also keeping the individual group identities salient will minimise any risk of identity threat, which happens when individuals feel their unique identity is being subsumed within a larger group (Dovidio et al., 1998; Hornsey & Hogg, 2000. Prasch et al., 2022). The dual identity model suggests a form of re-categorisation process for the original group so that the perceived threat can lead to a position where both the subordinate and superordinate identities are acknowledged and promoted simultaneously (Hogg, 2000). The message here for universities is not to lose sight of the individual's contributions when highlighting the organisation's goals and successes.

Within this dual identity model is a tension that Marginson (2000) flagged: A destructive stand-off between academic cultures and corporate management culture drives universities. Where we are now, the corporate management culture dominates the academic culture. Herein lies the tension for academics as the decline in public funding means alternate means of funding need to cover the shortfall, and this is where a corporate model seeks to fund the shortfall. Those that get promoted – and work within the system – "gain the benefits that come from obedience and passivity" (Cornell, 2019; p. 59).

Martela and Pessi (2018) examine the relationship between meaningfulness at work. They find that unification is key. Rosso et al. (2010) define it as actions that "bring individuals into harmony with other beings or principles", p.115. Thus, belongingness as interpersonal connectedness, closeness, and social identification with others at work is at the heart of the unification pathway. Pratt and Ashforth (2003) distinguish between meaningfulness in working and meaningfulness at work. Meaningfulness in work describes the degree to which the tasks and work are meaningful. And meaningful at work describes one's membership in the organisation and whom one surrounds oneself with as part of this membership. The last is a sense of agency over your work and the capacity to learn from your work. This creates belongingness and unification that closely align with the concept of meaningfulness at work.

Building that group identity goes a long way to finding your own identity. Discrimination means treating individuals differently depending on their social identity; prejudice means negative attitudes towards a particular social identity. In contrast, stereotypes are characteristics associated with people of social identity (Stangor, 2015). This categorisation helps us make sense of a complex world and make faster decisions, even though those decisions are often based on stereotypes. Naturally, we care more about those with whom we share a common group identity. We also tend to conform to the social norms of our groups because this strengthens our feeling of belongingness. Organisations can use social norms to motivate employees by making desirable norms salient.

Under these latter circumstances, group members may show reactance and increased motivation to achieve positive distinctiveness, consequently exacerbating intergroup bias. For example, Hornsey and Hogg (2000) found that a condition emphasising the common university identity of math-science and humanities students produced a higher level of bias than a condition that emphasised their separate group identities. In contrast, simultaneously emphasising superordinate and subgroup membership substantially reduced bias relative to both of these conditions.

Self-determination theory was developed by psychologists Richard Ryan & Edward Deci (2000), who studied school students' intrinsic and extrinsic motivations. They identified three universal desires: Autonomy, competence, and engagement. Because extrinsically motivated behaviours are not inherently exciting and thus must initially be externally prompted, the primary reason people are likely to be willing to do the behaviours is that they are valued by significant others to whom they feel (or would like to feel) connected, whether that be a family, a peer group, or a society they genuinely like, value, and trust. For example, faculty members in academia are often driven to collaborate and co-author with colleagues.

Various theories have emerged to explain the origins of intrinsic motivation. For instance, one line of research proposes that intrinsic motivation arises from aligning an individual's self-concept and a specific environment or activity (Deci & Ryan, 1985; Pinder, 1984). Then building on this cognitive perspective, self-determination theory suggests that the purest forms of motivation occur when individuals experience autonomy, competence, and relatedness in their endeavours (Deci & Ryan, 2000). When faculty members perceive intrinsic motivation in their work, it signals a congruence between their professional activities and their self-concepts, leading to a heightened sense of meaningfulness.

The key is to keep people curious, vital, and self-motivated; curious employees are more likely to be innovative and adaptable to the complexities of modern work and better job performance (Kashdan et al., 2020, Fry et al., 2024). Noted that research on life's meaning has shown how belonging contributes to meaningfulness (see Lambert et al., 2013). This emphasises a crucial distinction between the significance of life and meaningfulness at work. Life involves not only taking action but also the experience of "being alive", whereas work is viewed primarily as an action that individuals undertake.

Consequently, while being connected to a community through one's work may contribute to a sense of purpose in life, it is not typically the focus when evaluating the meaningfulness of one's job (Martela & Pessi, 2018). Locke and Taylor (1991) propose a cyclical process where personal values shape occupational choices, and the work experiences within those chosen fields reinforce and strengthen those values. The research and teaching that an academic is drawn to may provide intrinsic motivation and meaningfulness that aligns to their values. Perhaps traits such as curiosity, perseverance and critical thinking attract a certain type of person to academia.

Bringing the Group Together

It is important to consider the ways in which we can maintain our authentic academic identities in the multiplicity of communities that form an integral part of higher education institutional workplace settings. It is helpful to draw from the seminal framework of Maslow's Hierarchy of Needs (1943) to understand how an overall sense of wellbeing comes back to psychological and self-fulfilment needs. Maslow's Hierarchy of Needs suggests two physical needs, Psychosocial (air, water, food, warmth, and sleep) and Safety (security, shelter, and protection), and three non-physical needs, Belongingness (affection and acceptance), Esteem (self-esteem and esteem by others), and Self-Actualisation. The intention is that we move from the physical, at the base of the hierarchy, to the non-physical, at the top. In our context we focus on the three, non-physical, needs at the top of the hierarchy, beginning with belonging.

Belonging

When individuals develop a sense of belonging within their community and, more importantly, in their social group, this helps build relationships and a system of social support that can help them withstand the pressures of work and life. In particular, identity helps to withstand stress and shield against adversity. This is particularly important in resisting the demands of an increasingly corporate structure at a university where business models have been designed for control and management rather than creativity and freedom (Connell, 2019). It is also taking note of the changing academic work that is modernising rapidly.

Self Esteem

Aligning with a group that reaffirms your core values and beliefs contributes to your self-worth and a feeling of accomplishment that you are respected within your professional community. But this also can affirm identity to the group they belong to, create a greater sense of self-esteem and self-worth. Finding the right academic community that resonates with your talents and capabilities and celebrates your achievements goes a long way to building that greater sense of self.

Self-Actualisation

Your contribution to the community is two-fold; there is a motivation to achieve for the group, which can help to deliver success for the group and, in turn, further create a sense of identity. Indeed, being part of a community such as an academic community where one can collaborate and produce better outcomes for an individual. Working towards a common goal as a group can build a community and a sense of purpose. For an academic, the impact or relevance their work had for other individuals, groups, or the wider environment is where the most significant satisfaction lies. This could be seen in the fulfilment of watching students graduate and understanding how that individual contributed to the knowledge. In turn, it creates opportunities where the academic can learn and grow and ultimately contribute to knowledge creation which is the core tenet of an academic.

Leadership Support

The influence of the leaders' and followers' personal histories and trigger events are considered antecedents of authentic leadership and followership, as well as the reciprocal effects with an inclusive, ethical, caring, and strength-based organisational climate. Positive modelling is viewed as a primary means whereby leaders such as university management and highly regarded professors develop authentic followers. There are simple steps to create a sense of belonging that needs to be reiterated. Jay Van Bavel and Packer (2021) have four suggestions (1) Think and talk like you care about the group – use inclusive language. (2) Use symbols that create an identity – think about sports teams and how their colours invoke a sense of belonging. (3) Reward collective performance – particularly unsung heroes who put the group first. (4) Finally, pay attention to social norms – within the group, we look to others to see how we should behave and create norms that signify success.

Conclusion

Identity is human nature. In a work setting, you need to understand who can help you achieve your goals to get the job done. Getting the job done for an academic means scholarship in research and teaching as well as service in administration and public engagement. However, the environmental elements that traditionally protected the academic against stress and burnout are being eroded – these changes to norms for autonomy, role clarity, and collegiality impact academic wellbeing. Given the changing nature of academic life, individuals need to understand their self-identity and who has their back to counter job dissatisfaction and to stay true to their beliefs and values.

Reflections from Chapter Author

I have worn various hats in my academic journey, each marking a distinct stage in my career (see reflection drawing, Figure 4.1). Initially, my focus was on teaching and learning, a role that gradually transformed from a part-time pursuit into a full-fledged career. With time, my emphasis shifted towards research, followed by a deep dive into engagement, encompassing leadership, and external collaborations with industry partners and media outlets.

Throughout these stages, my approach to collaboration evolved in tandem with my career trajectory. In the beginning, I sought guidance from mentors and established researchers, aiming to broaden my horizons. During the middle phases of my career, collaboration became more about working with individuals I resonated with, fostering an environment of openness and collaboration where I thrived. In the latter phase, my focus shifted towards mentoring and engagement, emphasising the importance of storytelling as a means to convey knowledge effectively, and ensure the most comprehensive impact of my research.

Curiosity and openness are central to my professional ethos, driving my continuous quest for learning and growth. These values have not only shaped my academic identity but have also been pivotal in the way I approach my work, fostering meaningful collaborations and impactful storytelling throughout my career.

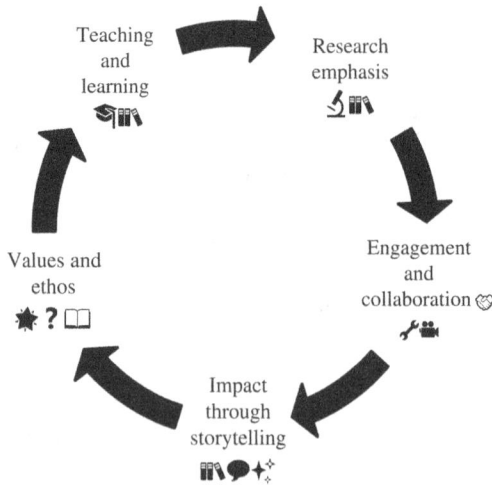

Figure 4.1 Reflection Drawing – My Personal Identity and Career Narrative

References

Albert, S., Whetten, D. A., Cummings, L. L., & Staw, B. M. (1985). Organizational identity. *Revealing the corporation: perspectives on identity, image, reputation, corporate branding, and corporate-level marketing: an anthology*, 77–105.

Bohnet, I. (2016). *What works*. Harvard University Press.

Bourdieu, P. (1980). *The logic of practice*. Stanford University Press.

Clair, J. A., Beatty, J. E., & Maclean, T. L. (2005). Out of sight but not out of mind: Managing invisible social identities in the workplace. *Academy of Management Review*, *30*, 78–95.

Connell, R. (2019). *The good university: What universities actually do and why it's time for radical change*. Bloomsbury Publishing.

Debowski, S. (2007). Challenges and dilemmas for Australian academics. *HERDSA News*, *29*(3), 21.

Deci, E. L., & Ryan, R. M. (1985). Conceptualizations of intrinsic motivation and self-determination. In Deci, E. L., & Ryan, R. M. (eds) *Intrinsic motivation and self-determination in human behavior, Springer, Boston, MA.*, (pp. 11–40). Springer. Boston, MA.

Deci, E. L., & Ryan, R. M. (2000). The "what" and "why" of goal pursuits: Human needs and the self-determination of behavior. *Psychological Inquiry*, *11*(4), 227–268.

Diehl, M. (1990). The minimal group paradigm: Theoretical explanations and empirical findings. *European Review of Social Psychology*, *1*(1), 263–292.

Dovidio, J. F., Gaertner, S. L., & Validzic, A. (1998). Intergroup bias: Status, differentiation, and a common in-group identity. *Journal of Personality and Social Psychology*, *75*(1), 109.

Erickson, R. J. (1995). The importance of authenticity for self and society. *Symbolic Interaction*, *18*(2), 121–144.

Fry, J., Elkins, M., & Farrell, L. (2024). Cognition and curiosity: Strategies for firms to recruit curious employees. *Applied Economics*, *56*(10), 1119–1135.

Goffman, E. (1963). *Stigma: Notes on the management of spoiled identity*. Prentice Hall.

Harris, S. (2005). Rethinking academic identities in neo-liberal times. *Teaching in Higher Education*, *10*(4), 421–433.

Haynes, K., & Fearfull, A. (2008). Exploring ourselves: Exploiting and resisting gendered identities of women academics in accounting and management. *Pacific Accounting Review*, *20*(2), 185–204.

Heidegger, M., Macquarrie, J., & Robinson, E. (1962). *Being and time*. Blackwell Publishing Ltd.

Hogg, M. A. (2000). Subjective uncertainty reduction through self-categorization: A motivational theory of social identity processes. *European Review of Social Psychology*, *11*(1), 223–255.

Hornsey, M. J., & Hogg, M. A. (2000). Assimilation and diversity: An integrative model of subgroup relations. *Personality and Social Psychology Review*, *4*(2), 143–156.

Jetten, J., Spears, R., & Manstead, A. S. (1996). Intergroup norms and intergroup discrimination: Distinctive self-categorisation and social identity effects. *Journal of Personality and Social Psychology*, *71*(6), 1222.

Kashdan, T. B., Disabato, D. J., Goodman, F. R., & McKnight, P. E. (2020). The five-dimensional curiosity scale revised (5DCR): Briefer subscales while separating overt and covert social curiosity. *Personality and Individual Differences*, *157*, 109836.

Lambert, N. M., Stillman, T. F., Hicks, J. A., Kamble, S., Baumeister, R. F., & Fincham, F. D. (2013). To belong is to matter: Sense of belonging enhances meaning in life. *Personality and Social Psychology Bulletin*, *39*(11), 1418–1427.

Locke, E. A., & Taylor, M. S. (1991). Stress, coping, and the meaning of work. In A. Monat, & R. S. Lazarus (Eds.), *Stress and coping: An anthology* (pp. 140–157). Columbia University Press.

Marginson, S. (2000). Rethinking academic work in the global era. *Journal of Higher Education Policy and Management, 22*(1), 23–35.

Marginson, S. (2007). University mission and identity for a post post-public era. *Higher Education Research & Development, 26*(1), 117–131.

Martela, F., & Pessi, A. B. (2018). Significant work is about self-realisation and broader purpose: Defining the key dimensions of meaningful work. *Frontiers in Psychology, 9,* 363.

Maslow, A. H. (1943). A theory of human motivation. *Psychological Review, 50*(4), 370.

Milkman, K. L., Akinola, M., & Chugh, D. (2015). What happens before? A field experiment exploring how pay and representation differentially shape bias on the pathway into organisations. *Journal of Applied Psychology, 100*(6), 1678.

Pinder, C. C. (1984). *Work motivation: Theory, issues, and applications.* Scott Foresman & Company.

Prasch, J. E., Neelim, A., Carbon, C. C., Schoormans, J. P. L., & Blijlevens, J. (2022). An application of the dual identity model and active categorisation to increase intercultural closeness. *Frontiers in Psychology, 13,* 705858.

Pratt, M. G., & Ashforth, B. E. (2003). Fostering meaningfulness in working and at work. In K. S. Cameron, J. E. Dutton, & R. E. Quinn (Eds.), *Positive organizational scholarship: Foundations of a new discipline* (pp. 309–327). Berrett-Koehler.

Rokeach, M. (1973). *The nature of human values.* Free Press.

Rosso, B. D., Dekas, K. H., & Wrzesniewski, A. (2010). On the meaning of work: A theoretical integration and review. *Research in Organisational Behavior, 30,* 91–127.

Ryan, R. M., & Deci, E. L. (2000). Intrinsic and extrinsic motivations: Classic definitions and new directions. *Contemporary Educational Psychology, 25*(1), 54–67.

Sahakian, B., & LaBuzetta, J. N. (2013). *Bad moves: How decision making Goes wrong, and the ethics of smart drugs.* OUP Oxford.

Schwartz, S. H. (2014). Rethinking the concept and measurement of societal culture in light of empirical findings. *Journal of Cross-Cultural Psychology, 45*(1), 5–13.

Schwartz, S. H., Cieciuch, J., Vecchione, M., Davidov, E., Fischer, R., Beierlein, C., & Konty, M. (2012). Refining the theory of basic individual values. *Journal of Personality and Social Psychology, 103*(4), 663.

Sprecher, S., Treger, S., Wondra, J. D., Hilaire, N., & Wallpe, K. (2013). Taking turns: Reciprocal self-disclosure promotes liking in initial interactions. *Journal of Experimental Social Psychology, 49*(5), 860–866.

Stangor, C. (2015). *Social groups in action and interaction.* Routledge.

Tajfel, H., Billig, M. G., Bundy, R. P., & Flament, C. (1971). Social categorisation and intergroup behaviour. *European Journal of Social Psychology, 1*(2), 149–178.

Tajfel, H., & Turner, J. C. (1979). An integrative theory of intergroup conflict. In W. G. Austin & S. Worchel (Eds.), *The social psychology of intergroup relations* (pp. 33–47). Monterey, CA: Brooks/Cole.

Tajfel, H. E. (1978). *Differentiation between social groups: Studies in the social psychology of intergroup relations.* Academic Press.

Van Bavel, J. J., & Packer, D. J. (2021). *The power of us: Harnessing our shared identities to improve performance, increase cooperation, and promote social harmony* (1st ed.). Little, Brown Spark.

Van Bavel, J. J., & Cunningham, W. A. (2009). Self-categorisation with a novel mixed-race group moderates automatic social and racial biases. *Personality and Social Psychology Bulletin, 35*(3), 321–335.

Webb, C. (2017). *How to have a good day.* Pan Macmillan.

Wood, A. M., Linley, P. A., Maltby, J., Baliousis, M., & Joseph, S. (2008). The authentic personality: A theoretical and empirical conceptualisation and the development of the authenticity scale. *Journal of Counselling Psychology, 55*(3), 385.

Chapter 5

Innovative Practices for Supporting and Promoting Academic Faculty Wellbeing in the Higher Education Sector – Abstract

Kate Hynes[1]

Introduction: The Challenges of Work-Life Balance and Wellbeing in Academia Today

Striking a balance between work and personal life can represent a challenge for many academics in higher education around the world.[2] In the past, academia was seen to offer a career within a low-pressurised work environment. However, in more recent years the tide has turned (Kinman, 2014). Bothwell (2018) reports findings from a major global survey of higher education faculty that long working hours are resulting in academics feeling stressed and struggling to fit time for relationships and family commitments around their increasing workloads. Those now working in academia are often working long hours by themselves, facing higher expectations to publish high-quality research regularly and to secure funding. "Publish or perish" is a term commonly used to describe the pressure to publish research to succeed in an academic environment. This encourages academics to act and live in ways that bring great benefits for the institution, but over time can lead to individuals burning out. Academics also face increasing pressure with high teaching loads and rising administrative burdens. Bakker and Demerouti (2007) outline how the Job Demands-Resource (JD-R) model can be applied to a wide range of professions and be used to improve employee wellbeing and performance.[3]

McDowall and Kinman (2017) examine the workplace culture of being "always on". Jarvenpaa and Lang's (2005) empowerment/enslavement paradox draws concerns about working anywhere, anytime can potentially lead to workers working everywhere all the time. Information and communication technologies (ICTs) linked to work can be associated with checking devices compulsively (Ter Hoeven et al., 2016) and multi-tasking, leading to unforeseen increases in workload (Chesley, 2014; Ter Hoeven et al., 2016), longer working hours (Fenner & Renn, 2010), and technostress (Tarafdar et al., 2007). Long, demanding hours at work and the growing prevalence of technology that permits work to be undertaken off campus can create an intense conflict with responsibilities and recuperation opportunities outside of work. These can include but are not limited to spending time with family

DOI: 10.4324/9781003284772-8

and friends, hobbies, self-care, and personal development (Bartlett et al., 2021). Trying to be the perfect employee and work colleague can take its toll (Reid, 2015). Therefore, we need to ask ourselves how we can see two candles burning brightly at the same time and not one at both ends. By that I mean, how can we manage work and non-work-related responsibilities in ways that we simultaneously feel fulfilled in both spheres?

My research in academia as an economist predominantly focuses on issues in international trade. My career has opened international doors for me and has given me the opportunity to work in universities across the following diverse set of countries: Ireland, Hong Kong SAR, Saudi Arabia, China, and North Korea. These experiences have allowed me to observe how traditions, cultures, beliefs, and illusion constraints impact the choices people make. One book I have found particularly useful is Kahneman (2011), whereby he breaks down our judgement and choice into two systems. System 1 is fast, intuitive, and emotional. It operates automatically and quickly, with little or no effort. System 2, on the other hand, is slower, more deliberate, and more logical. It is associated with focus and concentration. Kahneman (2011) discusses how most of our decisions result from System 1 thinking. Next, looking through a global lens, I will discuss how System 1 and System 2 can impact work-life balance and wellbeing in the higher education sector.

Section 1: System 1, System 2, and Illusion Constraints

System 1 is that portion of consciousness that is not in focal awareness at any given time. It involves the processes in the mind that are driven by our beliefs that occur automatically and are not available for reflection. It incorporates thought processes, memory, habits, motivation, and skills related to how we do things. It houses all our emotions and how we *choose* to feel about things, people, events, and situations. Lipton (2005) claims that up to 95% of our behaviour is governed by System 1: Our subconscious mind. Beliefs are "in the driving seat" of System 1. Kahneman (2011) challenges us to try to distinguish familiarity from facts. In his book he states that "a reliable way to make people believe in falsehoods is frequent repetition, because familiarity is not easily distinguished from truth" (p. 62). It is therefore important for us to understand that our beliefs are not necessarily facts. Another book that I found very insightful is Hicks and Hicks (2004), who further highlight that our beliefs are only thoughts that we continue to think of. When our thoughts become repetitive, we can become so familiar with them that we can be misled and interpret them as the truth. Overtime our beliefs can become deep rooted, they are often linked to our values, which then influence our opinions. Understanding that we can consciously decipher the thoughts we hold gives us the power to have control over what we believe.

Hofstede (1991) is another study I found useful. He conducted one of the most comprehensive studies of how values in the workplace are influenced by culture. An insight I obtained from working across a variety of cultures is that deep-rooted traditions, cultures, and beliefs can impact a large proportion of collective behaviour. When those around us all hold similar beliefs, we tend not to question things and often hold the belief that "that's just the way life is". Yet, if we immerse ourselves in another culture or work in an environment where multiculturalism and diversity exist, we can observe behaviours that are clearly different from those beliefs we have grown accustomed to. This offers the opportunity to re-evaluate our own beliefs. Multiculturalism and diversity are so important for that reason alone. They can lead to an appreciation of contrasting experiences and reflection on whether we live our lives by, and according to which we make our choices, are encouraging or deterring us from living the lives we want.

Examples of cultures, traditions, and beliefs at the community or country level:

China

- In China, it is not uncommon for employees to connect with each other on WeChat groups and to be contacted about work on this informal platform outside of work hours.
- Hierarchy is very prevalent at Chinese universities as it is in wider Chinese society. There is an obligation to do what is asked of you by a colleague in a higher position than you. For that reason, those working at a lower level can be asked to complete both work and non-work-related tasks.
- Saying no to a boss is not common practice in China.

Hong Kong SAR

- The "Lion Rock Spirit" in Hong Kong is consistent with their "can do" attitude and hard work ethic.
- The work environment in Hong Kong is very competitive.
- Hong Kong Confederation of Trade Unions found that 20% of Hong Kong employees work an average of 55 hours per week. Seven days a year of paid leave is standard.[4]

Saudi Arabia

- In Saudi Arabia, Muslims pray five times a day. Work comes to a halt during prayer times and hence the flow of productivity is also halted. Prayer determines the rhythm of the day.
- If something goes wrong in Saudi Arabia, for example, the IT doesn't work in the lecture hall, people have the attitude *Inshallah* (if Allah wills it).
- In Saudi Arabia, the campus buildings close for women at 4 pm. If you need to do work outside of these hours, you need to work from home. When working in a women's university, workmen cannot come on campus until all the women have left the building.[5]

North Korea

- North Koreans do not have high levels of trust in people from different countries. Foreign academic staff in North Korea need to submit their lecture notes prior to lectures as they need to be approved by the senior North Korean staff in the University.
- In North Korea, people's awareness of the outside world is curtailed due to the restrictive regime they are living under. This impacts the research academics are able to conduct and the content they teach their students.

France

- France passed a law that allows employees to disconnect from work emails outside work hours.
- In France workers get a minimum of five weeks paid vacation time. The law establishes the work week as 35 hours; nevertheless, overtime does occur.

Can you identify if your culture plays a major role in your work-life balance and wellbeing? If so, do you think it positively or negatively impacts it?

Judge et al. (1997) contributed to the literature by publishing a conceptual article linking an integrative personality trait termed Core Self Evaluations (CSEs) to job satisfaction.[6] They propose that CSEs are fundamental evaluations that individuals hold about themselves, the world, and others. CSEs are predominantly influenced by our past experiences, our family, and our peers.[7] We can often be unaware of our deep-rooted CSEs, but they impact so much of our perceptions, decisions, actions, and outcomes in our lives. Again, I must highlight that beliefs are not necessarily facts. Sometimes beliefs can be self-serving and assist us in moving closer to the way we want to live our lives, and sometimes they hinder us from doing so. An example of a CSE could be, "I am a capable and competent person". This belief is aligned with good self-efficacy. When an individual believes something can be accomplished, the mind will automatically begin creating ideas that will pave the path to success. There are barriers for an individual to grow and progress in life beyond the individual's level of belief. If an individual tries to achieve something beyond their level of belief, the mind will instantly and automatically create ideas or reasons rationalising why it can't be accomplished. For example, "I will never get promoted". Table 5.1 below outlines several CSEs. The first six listed are associated with positive CSEs while the latter six listed are associated with negative CSEs.

Illusion constraints are limitations an individual imposes on themselves based on a belief they hold. The distinction between legitimate constraints and illusion constraints is an important one. Legitimate constraints are fact-based constraints while illusion constraints are belief-based constraints. Reiterating Kahneman (2011), beliefs are not necessarily facts. When illusion constraints are impeding us from fulfilment, we can feel resistance and negative emotions.

Table 5.1 Core Self-Evaluation Exercise

	Do not believe	*Sometimes believe*	*Strongly believe*
I am naturally creative, resourceful, and whole.			
I am capable and competent.			
It's okay to make mistakes at work.			
My colleagues have good intentions and are doing the best they can with the knowledge and resources available to them.			
I can unwind and relax after work.			
I feel supported to bring forth new ideas in my workplace.			
I'm a failure if I'm not viewed as being perfect. I need my colleagues to think I'm perfect.			
I will become happy only when my research gets published in a top journal.			
I will never get promoted.			
I can't trust anyone; they will steal my ideas.			
I'm not good at using or learning new technologies.			
My self-esteem will only elevate if I (i) get good teaching evaluations, (ii) successfully win funding, or (iii) publish research in a top journal.			

Figure 5.1 illustrates how an illusion constraint leads to negative thoughts which result in negative feelings, this then drives unwanted actions and results.

However, with increased awareness and a change in perspective this illusion constraint can potentially transform or dissolve. Resistance can lessen, transform, or disappear when our awareness grows. When our beliefs become aligned with our wants, our expectations and actions also become aligned with our goal. Figure 5.2 illustrates how a having a positive conscious belief leads to positive thoughts and feelings, which then results in desired actions and results.

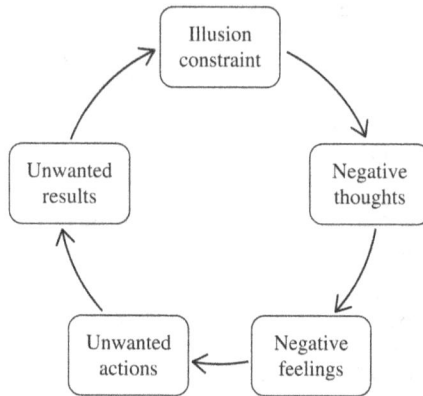

Figure 5.1 Illusion Constraint Feedback

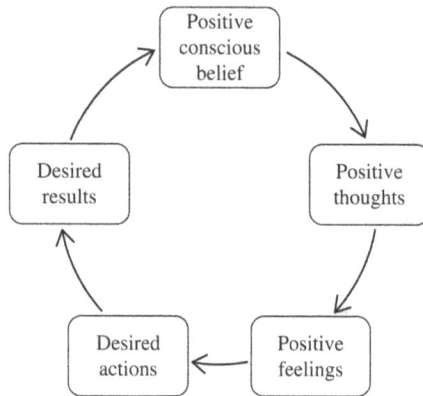

Figure 5.2 Positive Conscious Belief Feedback

Being aware of our beliefs and linking them to the emotions we feel about a particular subject in our lives is crucial if we want to raise our awareness and dissolve illusion constraints that are no longer self-serving. To identify illusion constraints, we need to become more aware of the inconsistencies our beliefs may have towards our goals. When your belief is integrated into your psyche and is aligned with your goals, your emotional state, thoughts, and actions all move in the direction of what you want. Some examples of illusion constraints, typical in academia that might be useful to consider are outlined below, in Table 5.2. It should be noted that this is one type of approach. It's not a universal fix all but is an element of achieving greater work-life balance satisfaction.

Table 5.2 Illusion Constraints Exercise

	Do not believe	Sometimes believe	Strongly believe
I need to work long hours to be productive.			
People will dislike me if I say no; I need to avoid confrontation at all costs.			
I will make my health a priority after I achieve a work target.			
I will reconnect and prioritise my time with family and friends after I complete a work commitment.			
I will do the things I love and start new hobbies after I accomplish my next work goal.			
I don't have time for volunteer work or similar commitments that are important and meaningful to me.			

Illusion Constraint 1: I need to work long hours to be productive.

Would you consciously choose this as your belief? What implications does this have for work-life balance and wellbeing? If this is an underlying belief for an individual, that individual will unconsciously work long hours irrespective of how productively they have been working. Illusion constraints can influence our behaviour, behaviour we would not consciously choose. Why would we consciously choose to allocate time to work unproductively? Yet, if I have a belief that *I need to work long hours to be productive* then an underlying feeling of guilt or worry will arise when I take time off from work, even from unproductive work. Such illusion constraints have resulted in the practice of overworking, fatigue, and stress which has mistakenly become normalised. Naturally, at times working longer hours may be required when you need to meet a deadline. However, if this is the relationship you automatically have with work then it is highly likely burnout will occur in the long run. This illusion constraint is in opposition to wellbeing and work-life balance. When we uncover an illusion constraint, we need to replace it with a conscious belief; for example, *I choose to work when I am working productively*. This conscious belief can be changed at any stage if it does not resonate. If a belief does not align with the way you want to live your life, you can change it to something that is better aligned. Feeling light and easy about our beliefs and being unattached from them allows us to update them as we see fit. When you feel at ease or positive emotions, you have greater access to thoughts that are more in alignment with what you want than when you feel negative emotions.

Illusion Constraint 2: People Will Dislike Me if I Say No; I Need to Avoid Confrontation at all Costs.

Overcoming this illusion constraint enables one to have the option of setting appropriate boundaries. Some people are very comfortable with setting boundaries and saying no when asked to do something that they do not want to do. Others may find it deeply uncomfortable to say no to another person. Do you put the needs and wants of another person ahead of your own work-life balance and wellbeing? An example of a conscious belief could be *Being assertive is a quality that I admire and embody*. Implementing boundaries around your work is essential for concentrating on the work you want to focus on and preventing work from dominating other areas of your life. If you feel you take on too much work and feel overwhelmed by this – make a conscious choice to not overcommit. Learn to say "no". A softer approach could be to say, "Unfortunately it's not feasible for me to take on this extra task right now" or "I'm afraid I won't be able to commit to doing this additional task within the timeframe you need". It's imperative to get the balance right. It's important that you focus on what is important to you but if this is done exclusively, organisations simply don't function effectively. Sole self-focus will also ultimately cut you off from key social support mechanisms. Balance is key.

Illusion Constraint 3. (a) I will make my health a priority when I achieve X; (b) I will reconnect and prioritise my time with family and friends when I achieve X; (c) I will do the things I love and start new hobbies when I achieve X.

X could represent work targets such as the next publication, successfully obtaining funding, getting promoted or finishing teaching/grading for the semester. Would you consciously choose to live life this way? Do you consciously believe that your health and lifestyle should be dependent on what you have achieved in your work-life?

Regarding (3a), making your health, self-care, and relaxation a priority is important and this should not only become important after you achieve a future goal. Sonnentag et al. (2022) highlights the important nature of unwinding and recovering from our working lives to sustain worker's wellbeing, motivation, and productivity levels. When we put something important to us on hold until after we accomplish something else, our goalposts will keep changing and it becomes unlikely that we ever accomplish it. Keeping your body and mind in a healthy condition can positively spill over to your productivity levels in work. An example of a conscious belief could be *My health and general wellbeing is very important to me.*

Regarding (3b), this illusion constraint can be a never-ending trap. If you keep putting off simple pleasures in life until you reach certain goals, you will find that the goal post will keep changing, and it becomes impossible to reach. Having a career in academia – or in any other industry for that matter – does not require a loss in the quality of your relationships. Arranging to connect with those you care about in advance of the meeting will create a commitment that may make it more difficult to cancel plans instead of sitting at your desk working productively or unproductively. Connecting with family and friends to spend time together can be both simple and highly fulfilling.[8] An example of a conscious belief could be *Spending quality time with my family and friends is a priority to me.*

Regarding (3c), spending time doing hobbies or exploring new hobbies should be part of our everyday lives (Powell (2017), Woolston (2015)). This could be playing sports or musical instruments, dancing, hiking, going for walks, spending time in the gym, taking cooking lessons, being out in nature, listening to music, gardening, etc. Prioritising activities that get you into your body and out of your head can assist an individual's motivation and focus. It promotes creativity and productivity. It can bring about high levels of satisfaction and feelings of accomplishment. An example of a conscious belief could be *I have more energy when I am doing the things I love to do.*

Section 2. Exercises to Assist in Gaining More Awareness About Our Beliefs[9]

Do you expect an individual's beliefs to be the same or change as they experience more in life? For instance, do you think an individual has the same beliefs about their own self-esteem or self-efficacy across their whole career? Do you think an individual has the same beliefs when they were a PhD student, Assistant Professor, Associate Professor, or full Professor? Or do you think these beliefs change over time and as we expand our awareness in both our work and personal lives? It is healthy for the beliefs we hold about ourselves and how the world around us operates to change as our lives become more enriched with new experiences and interactions. Regularly doing a house clean of your beliefs about areas of life that matter to you is a healthy practice. By "house clean" I mean identifying if the thoughts you continue to think about focus on (1) the positive emotions of having or embodying that which you want or (2) the negative emotions from the absence or lack of not having it in your life. If your answer is (1), then your beliefs are likely to be in alignment with the way you want to live your life. If your answer is (2), then your beliefs are likely to be in opposition to what you want, and it may serve you well to re-frame how you think about this subject matter. To be aware of where your focus and attention goes is of the utmost importance. We so often become what we focus on.

Another book I found useful is Branden (1994). In it, he discusses how he uses sentence completion work as a powerful tool for raising self-understanding, self-esteem, and personal effectiveness. He states that this practice

> … rests on the premise that all of us have more knowledge than we normally are aware of – more wisdom than we use, more potentials than typically show up in our behaviour. Sentence completion is a tool for accessing and activating these hidden resources.
>
> (Branden, 1994, p. 84)

He acknowledges that sentence completion work can be used in many ways and describes a way he finds most effective. First, he recommends writing down an incomplete sentence, and to keep adding at least six different endings. The main requirement being that each ending be a grammatical completion of the sentence. We should write these endings as quickly as possible to ensure we don't stop to *"overthink"* about the task. Let's now use this technique to facilitate the process of learning to live a life with more work-life balance and wellbeing, Table 5.3.

Table 5.3 Practicing Work-Life Balance and Wellbeing Exercise

Wellbeing in my life looks like
Wellbeing in my life looks like
Wellbeing in my life looks like
Wellbeing in my life looks like
Wellbeing in my life looks like
Wellbeing in my life looks like
If I consider where I struggle to practice wellbeing, I will
If I consider where I struggle to practice wellbeing, I will
If I consider where I struggle to practice wellbeing, I will
If I consider where I struggle to practice wellbeing, I will
If I consider where I struggle to practice wellbeing, I will
If I consider where I struggle to practice wellbeing, I will
If I bring a higher level of consciousness to the areas where I struggle to practice wellbeing, I will
If I bring a higher level of consciousness to the areas where I struggle to practice wellbeing, I will
If I bring a higher level of consciousness to the areas where I struggle to practice wellbeing, I will
If I bring a higher level of consciousness to the areas where I struggle to practice wellbeing, I will
If I bring a higher level of consciousness to the areas where I struggle to practice wellbeing, I will

(Continued)

Table 5.3 (Continued)

If I bring a higher level of consciousness to the areas where I struggle to practice wellbeing, I will

If I bring more wellbeing to my work, I will

If I bring more wellbeing to my work, I will

If I bring more wellbeing to my work, I will

If I bring more wellbeing to my work, I will

If I bring more wellbeing to my work, I will

If I consider my wellbeing to be a high priority, I will

If I consider my wellbeing to be a high priority, I will

If I consider my wellbeing to be a high priority, I will

If I consider my wellbeing to be a high priority, I will

If I consider my wellbeing to be a high priority, I will

If I consider my wellbeing to be a high priority, I will

Emotional wellbeing refers to the awareness and understanding of our emotions and how well we can manage our emotions through different circumstances in life. Hicks and Hicks (2004) developed the Emotional Guidance Scale (EGS). Table 5.4 illustrates the EGS and offers a sequence of commonly felt emotions ranging from the highest vibration to the lowest vibration.[10] Our thoughts and feelings are closely linked to each other.

When you would like to feel better about a particular subject in your life (for example, work, teaching, research, relationships, health, hobbies, finances), you can identify where you currently are on the EGS in relation to that domain. Reaching for thoughts that you have access to that feel slightly better can support you

Table 5.4 The Emotional Guidance Scale

1. Joy/Knowledge/Empowerment/Freedom/Love/Appreciation
2. Passion
3. Enthusiasm/Eagerness/Happiness
4. Positive Expectation / Belief
5. Optimism
6. Hopefulness
7. Contentment
8. Boredom
9. Pessimism
10. Frustration/Irritation/Impatience
11. Overwhelm (feeling overwhelmed)
12. Disappointment
13. Doubt
14. Worry
15. Blame
16. Discouragement
17. Anger
18. Revenge
19. Hatred/Rage
20. Jealousy
21. Insecurity/Guilt/Unworthiness
22. Fear/Grief/Depression/Despair/Powerlessness

in moving up the EGS and help you feel better. Bernstein (2019) highlights how effective this strategy is in assisting people to think and feel better about different areas of their life. She also acknowledges that we can naturally move up the EGS when we become distracted by something that makes us feel better than the negative thoughts we previously focused on.

This practice can be done as follows: write your thoughts down in Table 5.5, write a few sentences about how you feel about a particular area of your life. You can write about what has occurred but, more importantly, you should describe how you feel. Then write an additional statement that clarifies precisely how you feel. Identifying this will assist you more easily to acknowledge any enhancement as you move through the process.

For example: Not getting promoted at work

Initial thoughts could include thoughts of powerlessness and insecurity emotions 22 and 21 on the emotional scale.

Regardless of how dedicated I am to the work I do; I still haven't been promoted.

I feel as though I'll never move up the career ladder because I've already done everything I can do, and I still didn't get promoted.

It seems there are many unfair variables at play in the promotion process which I don't understand.

Table 5.5 Writing Exercise

Step 1. Write down what has occurred.

_____

_____

_____

_____

_____

Step 2. Describe how you feel.

_____

_____

_____

_____

_____

Step 3. Write a statement clarifying how you feel.

_____

_____

_____

_____

_____

Step 4. Reach for better feeling thoughts you have access to that bring you slightly higher on the EGS. Write these thoughts down.

_____

_____

_____

_____

_____

Even though you could be justified in how you are thinking and feeling, the current thoughts are low on the EGS. If we continue to ruminate on the same thoughts our emotions will get stuck in a negative spiral. When you're thinking negative thoughts and feeling negative emotions, high-vibe thoughts won't resonate, they would likely feel forced and false. A more suitable approach would be to gently guide yourself to consciously choose better feeling thoughts you have access to that can help you move up the scale step by step.

Better feeling thoughts

I should have been promoted.

It's so unfair. Everyone knows I have all the qualifications and experience necessary for this promotion.

I ought to quit my job. Then we'll see how they would cope without me.

Then it'll be clear to everyone who has been keeping this place together all this time.

Ah the sweet feeling of revenge! Although your colleagues or friends won't want to see you in a state of revenge or anger, these emotions do feel better than powerlessness. Even though these are still negative emotions, there is an improvement and an upward movement on the EGS to emotions 19, 18, and 17. Let's continue with this process and reach for better feeling thoughts.

Better feeling thoughts

I know I am better than they think I am.

I will show them over the next year so they will really notice me.

I'm disappointed but not completely discouraged as I strive to be noticed.

You are continuing to move up the EGS, these are thoughts associated with the emotion disappointment.

Better feeling thoughts

I understand that I have many colleagues at work who work hard and are also deserving of a promotion.

If I'm being honest with myself, I don't really want to quit. I'll give it another year.

I can make the most of the situation I'm in.

I can observe my colleagues who recently got promoted and look for characteristics that could have made the difference.

With more consideration, I'm possibly not ready for the additional responsibilities that would have come with that promotion.

I feel how my awareness has expanded from this experience.

I'm fairly content with my current situation.

I feel enthusiastic about what my future holds.

I'm feeling eager to learn and grow from this experience.

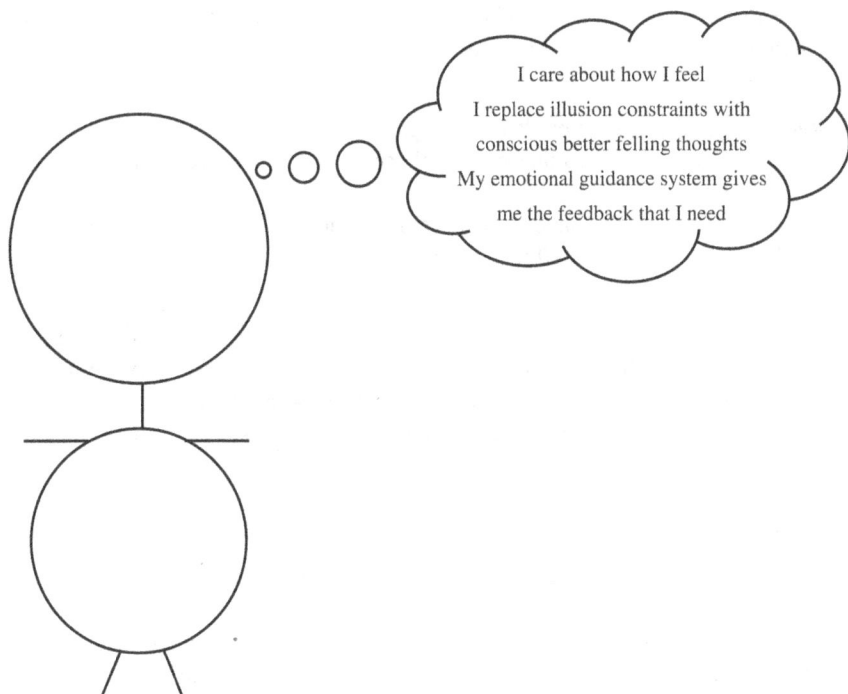

Figure 5.3 Prioritising Thoughts and Feelings That Feel Satisfying

Figure 5.3 offers an illustration that highlights that choosing the most satisfying thoughts you have access to will assist you in feeling as best you can in any given moment.

Section 3. Other Practices to Bring Forth Wellbeing and Work-Life Balance

Wellbeing Within an Increasing Digitalised Workplace

As our lives and workplaces become more reliant and intertwined with technology, it can sometimes distract us from what we want to be focused on. The movement to more online classes and asynchronous learning has made it difficult for some academics to switch off from the digital world. This increased pressure to perform online tasks can potentially impact our mental, emotional, and physical wellbeing, which may result in a reduction in our productivity levels. I have found it useful to become more digitally aware, recognising the possible harm that overuse of technological devices and applications can cause, whether it's shortening my attention spans or negatively influencing relationships or harming my productivity. Fatigue and mental tiredness can be a result of the following:

- Receiving and checking endless notifications.
- Periods of mindless scrolling on social media even on professional sites such as LinkedIn.
- Feeling the pressure to have a presence online and on social media.
- Having the urge to read and reply to countless emails, even on your time off.

The absence of a strong boundary, and an ability to switch off from the digital world, can influence how much we work and how we spend our leisure time. An important question we should all pose to ourselves: What practices can we implement once digital use becomes detrimental to our wellbeing? Some helpful practices include the following:

- Utilising the night mode option.
- Buy an alarm clock and leave your phone in another room when you sleep at night.
- Setting time limits for apps and websites can help you to become more conscious of the amount of time you spend on them (Wu et al., 2015).
- Pausing notifications and certain apps can allow you to retain your focus on what you consciously want to focus on.
- Schedule digital detoxes regularly.
- When spending time with others, try to offer them your full attention and not give into the tempting feeling of checking or using your phone.

Maintaining Separateness From Work When You Are Not Working

Some academics may find it difficult to take time off work. They may be involved in many research projects with different people, or be on management boards, supervising theses etc., and struggle to put up a boundary of switching off from all work-related tasks when they are on annual leave. When an individual takes time off work they should be completely switched off from it. Maintaining work-life balance and creating an emotional and mental separateness when away from work should be viewed as a prerequisite to living a healthy lifestyle. It also creates space to have enthusiasm and energy for work again when one returns to work after taking a break. Sustaining balance in our lives is essential for greater creativity and productivity levels. In addition to that, balance sets the stage for long-term fulfilment with work.

Rosen (2018) emphasises the importance of undertaking activities that bring joy to your life. Returning to basic lifestyle factors and the influence these basic lifestyle factors can improve people's physical, emotional, and mental health. These activities could include, but are not limited to the following:

- Spending time outdoors.
- Spending time in nature.
- Spend time with people you care about.
- Gardening, painting, dancing, playing sports, listening to music, reading, travelling.
- Meditating.
- Cooking healthy food.

Meditation and Mindfulness Exercises

The fundamental nature of meditation is to guide the focus of your attention to become deeply conscious of the present moment. I found by doing this, I can move my consciousness away from mental activity and instead be in a place where I am aware and alert in the absence of thinking. Brown et al. (2007) recognises that an individual's present-moment awareness can take on different forms, such as body sensations, emotional reactions, mental images, mental talk, sounds and perceptual experiences. In your daily life, you may find it helpful to practice this by offering your entire attention to a routine activity. This calls for you to be highly attentive to each of your senses; every movement, every breath, being completely present. The level of peace that an individual feels within from doing this practice is the main measure of its effectiveness. Jamieson and Tuckey (2017) review 40 published articles of mindfulness interventions in the workplace to identify ways in which these interventions in the workplace could be improved. Overall, they find the research suggests that mindfulness interventions are a useful resource for facilitating a range of aspects of employee health and wellbeing.

Meditation and mindfulness can lower stress levels, enhance creativity and productivity, and help in gaining higher levels of self-awareness and assist in concentrating your thoughts (Cannizzo et al., 2019; Creswell, 2017).[11] Becoming aware of your feelings can help you identify what you need in the moment. For instance, if you are feeling stressed maybe about your upcoming teaching evaluations or the research paper currently under review etc., it could be helpful to take a step away from what you are doing and go out for a brisk walk or do some stretches or meditation. Listening to what your body, mind, and soul needs in that moment is important. By doing something positive for yourself at that point in time can potentially help you through it. This is an excellent habit to get into and will help you in the long run.

Conclusion

This chapter acknowledges that although universities should monitor academics' wellbeing, there are a number of ways academics can help themselves – which requires frequent reflection and high levels of self-awareness. This starts with the knowledge that your beliefs are not necessarily facts; rather they are only thoughts that you continue to think of, and thus, become ingrained in your mind. Becoming more conscious of the impact of our culture, traditions, and CSEs is the first step. Identify which of these serve you and which are illusion constraints acting as barriers from living the life you would consciously choose for yourself. Sometimes illusion constraints keep someone in an unhealthy holding pattern of behaviour potentially causing negative emotions and behaviours.

There is no rule that fits for all. You will need to see what works best for you. Some may need to lean more into work and to try and create more dedicated time for productive working. Others may need to re-balance and dedicate more quality time for their personal and social lives. We need to care about how we feel. This should be our top priority. We can improve the way we feel by becoming more aware of our EGS and reach for better feeling thoughts that are associated with emotions slightly higher on the scale than we currently stand. Reaching for better feeling thoughts we have access to, will naturally bring about better feeling emotions.

For some, it may be important to set strong boundaries to ensure they have the right environment to work in. Being persistent in this can help create a productive space to work in. It may be helpful for some to become more mindful and discerning in how they are using technology in their daily lives, to maintain separateness from work when not working, and to do meditation and mindfulness exercises.

Reflective Paragraph

Writing this book chapter helped me reflect on my journey in academia and the challenges and celebrations of navigating my own work-life balance and wellbeing. Working in universities across different countries and cultures brought about the realisation that a few illusion constraints were standing in my way of living the life I wanted for myself. Personally, I wanted to manage my work and non-work-related responsibilities in ways that simultaneously made me feel fulfilled in both areas. However, I was used to unconsciously overworking (not always productively) and saying yes to more things than I could handle. How could I bring about new work patterns that were in opposition to the way I was operating for so many years? It was a gamechanger when I discovered that my emotional guidance system could give me the feedback that I needed. I made it my dominant intention to care about how I feel. This shift helped me refocus my thoughts in the direction of my desired results. At the start, this was trial and error. Meditation practices helped quieten my mind and focus my attention. My emotions give me feedback whether I am on or off track. I realise that this is a journey. Sometimes I will be off track, and when this happens, I remind myself that my emotions are my lighthouse (See Figure 5.4). I then prioritise how I feel and reach for the best feeling thoughts I have access to in that moment, which helps me move in the direction of being on track again.

Figure 5.4 Reflection Drawing – My Emotional Lighthouse

Notes

1 I would like to thank Edel Conway, Yseult Freeney, Patrick Hynes, Sinead Kelleher and Amanda Kelly for their helpful comments and suggestions.
2 In addition to what institutions can do to improve wellbeing among its employees, this chapter focuses on some practices the individual can implement.
3 Harney et al., (2018) use the JD-R model to investigate the impact of restructuring and downsizing on employee wellbeing.
4 Reported in South Morning China Post (see, Zhao, 2019).
5 I observed these behaviours in Saudi Arabia in 2016. There may have been changes to the university rules since then.
6 I will use the terms CSEs and beliefs interchangeable throughout the chapter.
7 O'Donoghue et al. (2016) find that abusive supervision negatively impacts employee wellbeing and is positively related to employee burnout. Their study also finds that employees low in CSE are less satisfied and less engaged than employees high in CSE.
8 It should be noted that not every academic has total freedom to make choices that are about putting themselves first. For instance, an individual may have caring demands. Rothbard et al. (2021) take a deeper delve into how depletion can occur when competing demands from different domains collide.
9 These exercises can be done in all areas of our life (for e.g., finances, health, relationships, physical and general wellbeing etc.) to help gather more awareness about our beliefs. There is no one size fits all rule for the exercises discussed in this section. The reader should only work through an exercise if it resonates with them, and they feel better in the process of doing it.

10 Bernstein (2019) also published the EGS in her book *Super Attractor* on page 66.
11 Creswell (2017) evaluates the growing evidence of mindfulness interventions in randomised controlled trials (RCTs) by focusing on the effects on health and interpersonal outcomes, dosing considerations, and the potential risks of interventions. This review highlights that some RCTs have shown to improve outcomes in the areas of chronic pain, depression relapse and addiction.

References

Bakker, A. B., & Demerouti, E. (2007). The job demands-resources model: State of the art. *Journal of Managerial Psychology*, *22*(3), 309–328.

Bartlett, M. J., Arslan, F. N., Bankston, A., & Sarabipour, S. (2021). Ten simple rules to improve academic work-life balance. *PLOS Computational Biology*, *17*(7), 1–12.

Branden, N. (1994). *Six pillars of self-esteem: The definitive work on self-esteem by the leading Pioneer in the field*. Bantam.

Bernstein, G. (2019). *Super attractor*. Hay House.

Bothwell, E. (2018). Work-life balance survey 2018: long hours take their toll on academics. *Times Higher Education*. https://www.timeshighereducation.com/features/work-life-balance-survey-2018-long-hours-take-their-toll-academics

Brown, K. W., Ryan, R. M., & Creswell, J. D. (2007). Mindfulness: Theoretical foundations and evidence for its salutary effects. *Psychological Inquiry*, *18*(4), 211–237.

Cannizzo, F., Mauri, C., & Osbaldiston, N. (2019). Moral barriers between work/life balance policy and practice in academia. *Journal of Cultural Economy*, *12*, 251–264.

Chesley, N. (2014). Information and communication technology use, work intensification and employee strain and distress. *Work, Employment and Society*, *28*(4), 589–610.

Creswell, J. D. (2017). Mindfulness interventions. *Annual Review of Psychology*, *68*(1), 491–516.

Fenner, G. H., & Renn, R. W. (2010). Technology-assisted supplemental work and work-to-family conflict: The role of instrumentality beliefs, organizational expectations, and time management. *Human Relations*, *63*(1), 63–82.

Harney, B., Fu, N., & Freeney, Y. (2018). Balancing tensions: Buffering the impact of organisational restructuring and downsizing on employee well-being. *Human Resource Management Journal*, *28*(2), 235–254.

Hicks, E., & Hicks, J. (2004). *Ask and it is given: Learning to manifest your desires*. Hay House.

Hofstede, G. (1991). *Cultures and organizations: Software of the mind*. McGraw-Hill.

Jamieson, S. D., & Tuckey, M. R. (2017). Mindfulness interventions in the workplace: A critique of the current state of the literature. *Journal of Occupational Health Psychology*, *22*(2), 180.

Jarvenpaa, S. L., & Lang, K. R. (2005). Managing the paradoxes of mobile technology. *Information Systems Management*, *22*(4), 7–23.

Judge, T. A., Locke, E. A., & Durham, C. C. (1997). The dispositional causes of job satisfaction: A core evaluations approach. *Research in Organizational Behavior*, *19*, 151–188.

Kahneman, D. (2011). *Thinking, fast and slow*. Macmillan.

Kinman, G. (2014). Doing more with less? Work and wellbeing in academics. *Somatechnics*, *4*, 219–235.

Lipton, B. H. (2005). *The biology of belief: Unleashing the power of consciousness, matter, and miracles*. Hay House.

McDowall, A., & Kinman, G. (2017). The new nowhere land? A research and practice agenda for the "always on" culture. *Journal of Organizational Effectiveness: People and Performance*, *4*(3), 256–266.

O'Donoghue, A., Conway, E., & Bosak, J. (2016). The influence of experienced abusive supervision on employee well-being and the buffering effect of employee core self-evaluations. In N. M. Ashkanasy, C. E. J. Härtel, & W. J. Zerbe (Eds.), *Emotions and organizational governance* (pp. 3–34). Emerald Group Publishing.

Powell, K. (2017). Work–life balance: Break or burn out. *Nature, 545,* 375–377.

Reid, E. (2015). Embracing, passing, revealing, and the ideal worker image: How people navigate expected and experienced professional identities. *Organization Science, 26*(4), 997–1017.

Rosen, J. (2018). How a hobby can boost researchers' productivity and creativity. *Nature, 558,* 475–477.

Rothbard, N. P., Beetz, A. M., & Harari, D. (2021). Balancing the scales: A configurational approach to work-life balance. *Annual Review of Organizational Psychology and Organizational Behavior, 8,* 73–103.

Sonnentag, S., Cheng, B. H., & Parker, S. L. (2022). Recovery from work: Advancing the field toward the future. *Annual Review of Organizational Psychology and Organizational Behavior, 9,* 33–60.

Tarafdar, M., Tu, Q., Ragu-Nathan, B. S., & Ragu-Nathan, T. S. (2007). The impact of tech-nostress on role stress and productivity. *Journal of Management Information Systems, 24*(1), 301–328.

Ter Hoeven, C. L., van Zoonen, W., & Fonner, K. L. (2016). The practical paradox of technology: The influence of communication technology use on employee burnout and engagement. *Communication Monographs, 83*(2), 239–263.

Woolston, C. (2015). Leisure activities: The power of a pastime. *Nature, 523,* 117–119.

Wu, X., Tao, S., Zhang, Y., Zhang, S., & Tao, F. (2015). Low physical activity and high screen time can increase the risks of mental health problems and poor sleep quality among Chinese college students. *PLoS One, 10*(3), e0119607.

Zhao, S. (2019, 14 April). *Long working hours: 1 in 5 Hong Kong employees are on the job an average of 55 hours per week, new trade union study shows.* South Morning China Post. Available at: https://www.scmp.com/news/hong-kong/hong-kong-economy/article/3006116/long-working-hours-1-5-hong-kong-employees-are-job

Chapter 6

Individual Wellbeing Practices for a Post-Pandemic University

Jonathan Boymal, Sam Sterling, Craig Williamson, Ying Zhou, and Patrick Lynch

Introduction

Universities are complex workplaces with the role of academics often being multi-faceted in nature, requiring diverse skillsets and excellence in what can sometimes be quite disparate areas (i.e., teaching and research) (see Figure 6.1). The academic role also comes with high expectations- often levelled by the academics themselves (it is a field that attracts high achievers) and a common stressor discussed on campus, especially of late, is the fast pace of change in higher education (Channing, 2022; Christiansen, 2022; Guppy et al., 2022). The inability to properly plan for, prepare for, and execute adeptly, the different parts of the role, is affecting the wellbeing of our academic colleagues (Gewin, 2021).

While the primary role of an academic remains teaching and research, the roles have now evolved to include many other aspects as well- such as leadership, administration, and external engagement- leading to even more competing priorities. It has been well studied that the demands of the job can be stressful, and it can be exceedingly difficult for academic staff to manage workloads and maintain a healthy work-life balance (Bell et al., 2012; Fetherston et al., 2021). The resulting pressures of this can lead to academic burnout (Urbina-Garcia, 2020; Vesty et al., 2018).

In acknowledging the complexities of the academic role, it is also important to understand the higher education workplace context – and the connection between the complexities outlined above and the wellbeing of staff. Osam et al. (2020) identify that, in the higher education context, psychological climate, engagement, and wellbeing are positively associated with each other, and engagement mediates the relationship between psychological climate and wellbeing. With engagement playing such an important role in higher education workplaces, this chapter will discuss academic engagement strategies as clearly central to ensuring academic wellbeing. The timeliness of this discussion is noteworthy, as pandemic-imposed changes, some now accepted as the new "business as usual", have directly impacted the ability of higher education educators to engage with each other – and with institutions – as they now largely teach online, research from home, and communicate from behind masks, or facelessly, with cameras off in virtual meetings. Bearing in mind the Osam et al. (2020) finding that engagement mediates the relationship between

DOI: 10.4324/9781003284772-9

Figure 6.1 Overwhelmed in Academia – the Mental Health Impacts of Academic Isolation

Source: Co-created with Adobe Photoshop

our psychologically complex academic environments and our wellbeing, it is clear that the impact of COVID-19 has been to expand the distance we need to bridge to ensure positive wellbeing in academia.

This chapter will explore the workplace practices, policies, and programmes that can support the engagement – and therefore wellbeing – of academics in higher education, with particular emphasis on career progression and negotiating daily academic roles.

Approaches to Academic Wellbeing

Academic wellbeing is of growing concern in both scholarly literature and social media. Existing studies on the wellbeing of academic staff *either* investigate the relationship between wellbeing and job factors, such as satisfaction, productivity, innovation, work engagement, turnover, and organisational performance (Bell et al., 2012; Jia et al., 2022; Mudrak et al., 2018; Taberner, 2018); or focus on the stressors experienced by specific groups, such as early career researchers, Higher Degree by Research (HDR) supervisors, non-tenure track faculty, and educators within a particular disciplinary field (Miner et al., 2019; Seipel & Larson, 2018; Vesty et al., 2018; Wisker & Robinson, 2016). Less is known about workplace practices that aim to enhance the wellbeing of academic staff as an objective in itself, or the implication of this on fostering a sustainable academic environment.

As the COVID-19 pandemic imposes an extra layer of intensity and complexity to the nature and structure of academic work (Christiansen, 2022; Guppy et al., 2022), the psychological wellbeing of academic staff has rapidly become a topic of broad global significance that requires not only a theoretical-empirical approach to examining wellbeing of academics as a means of achieving better workplace productivity and efficiency, but also an orientation towards the attainment of wellbeing of academics as an end in itself.

Therefore, the approach taken in this chapter is to apply a well-known framework for understanding an individual's wellbeing – the Ryff scale of psychological wellbeing (Ryff, 2014; Ryff & Keyes, 1995) – to the higher education context. The Ryff scale is widely used in positive psychology (Stavraki et al., 2022; Van Dierendonck & Lam, 2022) and identifies six factors that are important to a sense of personal wellbeing, namely purpose in life, self-acceptance, environmental mastery, autonomy, positive relationships and personal growth. In applying these six factors to the higher education workplace context, we consider Sorensen et al.'s (2021) expanded conceptual model for understanding and attributing proportionate value to measures that impact workplace safety, health and wellbeing, and apply these in practical terms to the modern academic workplace. In doing so, we identify the importance of promoting a two-tiered approach to enabling academics' engagement and wellbeing via both *formal* and *informal* actions. Finally, we discuss the inter-relation of actions that need to be taken by both organisations and individuals.

Issues in, and Solutions to, Academic Wellbeing

Framing academic workplace actions on wellbeing: The need for formal and informal measures that work together

Sorensen et al.'s (2021) expanded conceptual model explores the way in which workplace wellbeing policies, programmes and practices influence worker and organisational outcomes, and highlights the importance of considering both the internal workplace environment, and the broader, highly changeable, external conditions of work that cannot be divorced from these internal factors – such as the social/political/economic environment the organisation exists within, and specific labour and employment patterns that are exerting force on workers at any given moment in time. The overlaying of pressures highlighted in this model connect deeply with today's academic workplace context, as the complex internal university working environment is ensconced in layers of external complexities, such as the increased pace of technology uptake (Trevisan et al., 2020). This has raised the digital expectations of both the university and its future students. Additionally, the impact of the pandemic – which was felt particularly strongly in the university sector (Welch, 2022) – was further reducing job security and significantly changing relationships between universities and their government and industry stakeholders. This has resulted in more regular disruptions such as the oft-changing political and regulatory environments that impact the kinds of research and learning that are "in favour" (i.e., funded and promoted) at different times.

Therefore, applying Sorensen et al.'s (2021) expanded conceptual model to the university context provides us with opportunities to understand the importance, and proportional value, of utilising different approaches to workplace wellbeing in our university environs. Reflecting on the model in the higher education context brings into focus the importance of (a) taking immediate and ongoing actions to enhance wellbeing in academia, and (b) the need to enact this across multiple levels at once. As such, we are suggesting a two-tiered approach to enacting wellbeing solutions in academia, with those two tiers consisting of *informal* actions (taken by both the institution and the individual) to embed a culture of wellbeing and to frame mindsets and *formal* actions (in the form of policies, processes, and programmes) that it is incumbent on academic institutions to provide, and to academics to avail themselves of, to enable workplace health, productivity, and resilience through ongoing change. To see how this can work in reality, we will now address some specific, and common, issues in academia that can impact the wellbeing of staff.

Managing the Day-to-Day of Academic Roles

As previously noted, the university academic's role is multi-faceted (Jones & Weinrib, 2022), and requires continuous self-development around a constantly changing skillset. Here we explore how the complexities of the role impact on several of Ryff's aspects of positive functioning, namely: self-acceptance, environmental mastery, purpose in life (personal values), and personal growth.

Complexities of the Academic Role: Teaching versus Research

It has long been acknowledged in the higher education sector that some aspects of an academic's role are preferred. For example, research output is more likely to lead to promotion – particularly at the professorial level – than excellence in teaching (Riordan, 2011). However, this preference for research over teaching also results in cognitive dissonance with the day-to-day of the role, which generally revolves around teaching semesters and student satisfaction surveys. Marchant and Wallace (2013) refer to teaching as "low status work" (p. 61) and compare it to research labelled as "high status work" (p. 61) and while some may consider that to be an out-dated view of academia, others argue that it is still an extremely prevalent bias within the university sector, backed by both policy and procedure (Schimanski & Alperin, 2018). This disproportionate valuing of efforts expended impacts on an academic's self-image or self-acceptance (Ryff & Keyes, 1995). Having multiple, somewhat incongruent, aspects to your role creates pressures in and of itself; however, when these disparate role requirements are also valued differently by the institution, its students and external stakeholders (whose perspectives will differ depending on whether they are research partners or industry representatives looking to employ job-ready graduates) and your management, much confusion is created. What is the primary job role? The secondary role? This uncertainty impacts on an academic's ability to prioritise and be effective across competing priorities, impacting their opportunity for environmental mastery (Ryff & Keyes, 1995).

When wearing their researcher's hat, academics similarly face uncertainty regarding the value that may be placed on their area of disciplinary expertise at different times. Whole disciplines, and areas within them, can move in and out of public, political, or financial favour. The fluidity of the value proposition placed on your expertise, or area of passion, by your institute, external stakeholders, and/or those who fund your research can impact both self-image and environmental mastery – as it is harder to progress areas of research that are currently "out of favour" or not being funded. This issue can also cause a sense of isolation because it is harder to get, for example, your voice heard in the media, or to get your research into target journals when interest is elsewhere.

Another factor that impacts the sense of value the sector, and therefore the individuals in the roles, place on themselves is that of sessional teaching. Higher education institutions employ a large number of casual teaching staff, and these sessionals face permanent job uncertainty. On the one hand, the existence of a large, casualised workforce offers flexibility and opportunity for academics (to teach while completing their studies, to teach while working in industry), however, on the other, it results in a large group of staff with a sense of not being fully valued by the institution (Lema & Joullié, 2015) For example, there may be role limitations on sessional staff (i.e., they are often ineligible for coordinator or leadership roles).

There is additional pressure to take on a high teaching load in a given semester, because the course or class may not be available in subsequent semester/s. This results in a constantly changing routine, making work-life balance, and financial balance, difficult. Isolation is also increased for those sessional staff who generally have no office or defined space on campus, and who may not be invited to as many team meetings (as they aren't on salary), which often sees them just coming onto campus to teach their class and leaving again. Services and initiatives put in place by the university to support their staff, such as wellbeing leave, employee assistance programmes and initiatives that occur on campus, are either unavailable to sessional staff or less likely to occur in the (greatly reduced) time the staff member is actually present on campus. Issues facing sessional staff in particular, impact on Ryff's (2014) "personal growth" factor regarding career development, and a sense of fulfillment at work. Furthermore, these factors, as noted by Marchant and Wallace (2013) also have gendered implications due to the higher prevalence of women in teaching roles in higher education. Regardless of gender, however, this confusion or cognitive dissonance causes engagement to drop – or be spread thinly across competing priorities. In applying the Ryff framework, it is clear that impacts on both purpose in life (personal values) and, depending on the choices made and the path followed, personal (career) growth, are evident.

Formal and Informal Actions to Support Self-Acceptance, Environmental Mastery, Purpose in Life (Personal Values), and Personal Growth in Academic Settings

Perhaps the single most important lever that higher education institutions can pull in terms of supporting staff wellbeing, is to reduce the cognitive dissonance between the teaching and research interests of the organisation (and therefore its staff). It is clear to those of us who work in the teaching and learning field within Australian higher education institutions, that a cultural re-set is required. While many institutions are now moving to better reward and recognise teaching and learning expertise alongside research expertise, there is still a long way to go before we will see parity between these areas. For many years now, the teaching of students has been recognised as the core business of universities and a student-centred approach is the day-to-day norm. However, the concomitant repositioning of teaching as central to achieving such educational outcomes has largely been overlooked in this changing of the guard. Policies, workplace practices and, importantly, promotional cycles continue to preference research efforts over teaching efforts, and it is in these areas that changes need to be made. Parity of effort must be recognised in the institutional narrative, in the way that staff are engaged, promoted, and remunerated, and in the policies and procedures that govern the workplace.

In addition, formal approaches to wellbeing support, such as the provision of wellbeing leave, access to personal support (counselling, mental health advocacy), and including wellbeing as a standing agenda item for discussion in team meetings, are practices known to help academics manage role disparity and uneven workflows (Wray & Kinman, 2022). Informal approaches to supporting academics' wellbeing in relation to their role dichotomies can include providing opportunities for individuals to share their journey via attending or presenting at conferences, working on collaborative projects, or making time for shared scholarship and/or teaching projects.

Complexities of the Academic Role: Scope Creep

Over the past two decades, the expectations placed on academics have increased and diversified (Urbina-Garcia, 2020). This expansion of job roles is supported by a culture that rewards those who take on more responsibility, including leadership roles, involvement in projects and cross-functional deliverables, stakeholder engagement, industry currency, research development. However, each of these differing roles requires the development of new competencies, knowledge sets, and skills, and there is often limited training or instruction – academics, being intelligent people, are just expected to figure things out, thus creating real inefficiencies and additional pressures – and a reduction in what Ryff and Keyes (1995) refer to as "environmental mastery".

In Australia, the pandemic hit the university sector disproportionately hard, with border closures locking international students out of the country for extended periods (Littleton & Stanford, 2021). Being one of the few sectors that received no government support during this time, extreme tightening of budgets and mass job losses ensued. This has had ongoing effects in the university sector (Blackmore, 2020) and impacts especially hard on academics who are still required to produce the same outputs but now have far less resourcing and peripheral staffing to support them in these efforts. As more classes have moved online during this time, university systems designed for on-campus teaching have been less effective, new technologies have been introduced and thus the cycle of new skill development continues. The result of all this is that academics have had continuous, sustained impacts on their ability to master their environment.

Furthermore, the impact on self-image (who I am as an educator) – linked to Ryff's "self-acceptance" factor – has been significant. The high, and constantly changing, expectations that institutions have for their staff, particularly those in academic roles, are often exacerbated by an expectation that professional development related to job role efficiencies or new skill acquisition is not important, or not a good use of academics' time. Change management is often loosely applied, or similarly not given priority – the expectation being that university staff are smart, they will simply adapt. Intriguingly, as yet, the higher education sector in Australia has not focused its cutting-edge technology "smarts" on creating efficiencies for its own workforce (Zawacki-Richter et al., 2019), instead focusing those innovative approaches outwardly, solving other companies' problems. This leaves our time-poor academics to struggle on with inefficient and cumbersome administrative and reporting tasks, things that could easily have been automated and/or benefitted by the application of artificial intelligence, had they been prioritised for such focus.

Another example of the "scope creep" in academic roles relates to the impact of students' declining mental health. Increasingly, academics are observing growing numbers of students who are struggling through their studies with less-than-optimal mental health experiences. A 2019 study (reported in Machin, 2020) found that 36% of students sought help for anxiety or depression during their degree and this percentage will likely have increased significantly post-pandemic. Anecdotally, academics often report large numbers of students who are reluctant to turn their cameras on or interact with others in online classrooms and reflect on the fact that we just do not know what is going on for those students that we do not see or hear from. Are they having a mental health issue, or just a bad hair day?

The large proportion of students who are facing mental health challenges not only elicits a caring response from academics – particularly when in a supervisory role – it also impacts their ability to educate those individuals and raises a raft of questions: what is the role of educators in addressing mental health issues that are impacting in the classroom? How do mental health concerns among students impact on the educator's ability to teach affected students, and what support can we put in place for both students and staff facing sub-optimal mental health?

This highlights once again how changing conditions lead to additional burden on academics, requiring additional knowledge, skills, and solutions- extending their expertise in different directions.

The various elements of scope creep covered above are just some examples of what is a very broad, and cumulative, problem. These constant learning curves and uncertainty, the incredible pace of change and, therefore, lack of time to adequately identify and develop the relevant skills to be high achieving in every aspect, can challenge the individual's sense of self-image. Knowing who they are (how they best teach, research, supervise, etc.) and how they fit into the ever-changing higher education landscape can be hard to reconcile at speed, and this impacts on Ryff's "self-acceptance" factor.

This kind of job role overwhelm causes academics to disengage from their workplace and their colleagues, as they madly try to keep up with their ever-increasing workloads. This increases the already high levels of individualism and isolation that can be evident in academia. One of Ryff's six factors for positive psychological outcomes is autonomy (Ryff, 2014); however, in the higher education sector, too much autonomy can also have negative effects on academics' wellbeing. Isolation and siloing can instead occur, impacting on one's ability to form, and access/ make use of, the "positive relationships" that Ryff also identifies as a key factor in wellbeing (Ryff & Keyes, 1995).

Formal and Informal Actions to Address Detractors to Self-Acceptance and Positive Relationships in Academia

Actions that individuals, and institutions, can take to support academic wellbeing relating to Ryff's factors of self-acceptance and positive relationships (as well as combating academic isolation) include recognising the importance of being able to focus on one (or several) areas of personal strength in the workplace, rather than expecting individuals to do it all. In academic contexts, this can be achieved *informally* by providing opportunities for staff with different skill sets (both academic and professional) to partner together to collectively meet goals; and *formally*, through workload models that recognise and weight the different elements of academic roles appropriately, with wellbeing as a lens in determining what "appropriate" looks like.

There are gaps to be researched here, in our tech-enabled post-COVID universities, to identify what can/should be done digitally, what can be done in partnership with professional staff and what really is/should be the core work of the academic? Now, more than ever before, it is imperative that we understand how institutions can provide better systems, more nuanced professional development and effective support to our academics to create efficiencies, recognise and reduce pain points.

While gaps exist, there is data to support the importance of peer mentoring (Goerisch et al., 2019) and collaborations (Kligyte, 2021), both in terms of formal mentoring programmes and informal peer support opportunities, to improve academic wellbeing. This approach is considered, in the collective experiences of the authors of this chapter, to be a key tool, and one that is not currently well utilised, for improving the wellbeing of higher education staff. As such, we provide an in-depth review of mentoring possibilities in the following section.

The Importance of Mentoring in Academic Contexts

Mentoring, both formal or informal, is a proven method to assist individuals develop and become acclimatised to their environment (Nuel et al., 2021). In the university context, mentoring has long been utilised as a professional development tool, particularly for early career academics or as a tool for promoting ethnographic diversity (Freeman & Kochan, 2019). Commonly, however, mentoring is an added extra, a further requirement – something that isn't factored into workloads – and as such, it falls off the agenda as times get busy. Therefore, to be sustainable in academia, mentoring approaches and outcomes need to be highly and explicitly advantageous for both mentor and mentee. One aspect of mentoring that is worth focussing on here is the personal wellbeing benefit that can be attributed to it. From the eudemonic perspective explored in this chapter, taking part in mentoring can provide psychological benefits by affecting Ryff's factors of environmental mastery, personal growth, positive relations with others, purpose in life and self-acceptance (Branand & Nakamura, 2017). Furthermore, we believe the value proposition for mentoring in higher education contexts can be further enhanced by considering a modified approach that tailors more specifically to the university environment. To this end, we suggest mentoring be reconceptualised as a team effort between mentor and mentee rather than an overly hierarchical endeavour, as outlined below.

Traditionally, mentoring is conceived as a relatively hierarchical and directive relationship in which mentees are provided advice and solutions by more knowledgeable and/or experienced mentors. The aim of mentoring is to foster personal and professional growth and to support people to be better at what they do (Hobson & van Nieuwerburgh, 2022). This definition can be reconceptualised for the university environment, which as noted previously, is an environment of constant change and re-skilling requiring even the most experienced academics to stay curious and keep learning. It is therefore likely that at different times, mentor and mentee relationships can flip depending on skillsets held and directions taken.

Recently, the concept of *mentoring with* as opposed to *mentoring of* colleagues has been articulated (Goerisch et al., 2019) and this provides a particularly useful framework for shared learning in the university context. The shared learning can occur as formal mentoring, where a colleague is attached to another to provide that formal support which allows them to assimilate into the new environment, understand how the school/faculty/university functions, and seek advice when needed. Alternatively, it could occur as informal mentoring, where colleagues work together on joint activities and projects or support each other through a shared developmental journey. Informal mentoring has been acknowledged by academics as particularly useful throughout the COVID-19 pandemic, with the need to adapt quickly to a different teaching environment.

For mentoring to be successful, the relationship between the mentor and mentee is key, where common views and values tend to be essential. Universities are multicultural entities with academics and students are not necessarily from the country the university is located. Mentoring then becomes intercultural, and in itself, this brings benefits and challenges (Glass et al., 2021). A challenge initially is what Bourdieu (cited in Huang, 2019) would classify as an issue of cultural capital, in that the person is not familiar with the educational context in Australia and therefore does not understand the subtleties or nuances of the tertiary education sector. Mitchell (2018) states that mentoring in a cross-cultural environment can result in mentees building a significant range of intercultural communication and people skills, including the ability to relate to others, providing constructive feedback and communicating effectively across cultures and organisational levels and boundaries.

Whether the mentoring approach is formal or informal, hierarchical or shared, the benefits of taking part extend both ways and improve the wellbeing of both mentor and mentee/s. Rosemary et al. (2015), identified tangible benefits from mentoring in academia which include: improved teaching skills, the intellectual challenge of working on issues which may take you into unfamiliar territory, recognition of expertise, motivation resulting from self-development and responsibility, shared satisfaction at the success of a colleague; reinforced knowledge of current practice, and opportunities for future collaboration. These tangible benefits correlate to increased wellbeing when viewed via the Ryff framework, supporting each participant's personal growth, positive relationships, self-acceptance and autonomy in their roles.

Academia, Wellbeing, and Targets for Change

Individual-level factors that can influence the wellbeing of those working in academia, such as their beliefs, attitudes and skills, are embedded within higher education institutions that exert considerable influence over the choices that staff make, their wellbeing practices, and the resources they have to aid them in those choices and practices. Sorensen et al.'s (2021) expanded conceptual model supports the view that organisational structures, policies and procedures, opportunities for career progression, organisational goals and management styles, informal social networks, physical working arrangements, job design and technology can directly and indirectly (through their impact on engagement and the wellbeing practices of those working in academia) influence the wellbeing of academic staff.

To address the issue of wellbeing in academia, we need to address the policies, practices and approaches that impact each day on our teams, our colleagues and ourselves. To this end, the application of Ryff's six factors for psychological wellbeing to the university context has been informative, providing a clear picture of where efforts can be focused for maximum impact. Table 6.1 summarises the

Table 6.1 Formal and Informal Actions to Support Wellbeing

Formal action	Informal action	In support of (Ryff factors)
Revise policies and procedures to provide parity of recognition for teaching cf. research efforts Ensure adequate change management that keeps pace with changing university dynamics and explicitly preferences the resultant professional development needs Access to personal support (e.g., wellbeing leave, counselling, mental health advocacy, career development) Institutions should make better use of tech tools to create efficiencies, allowing staff to focus on their key role/s (reduce administrative load etc.) Formalise the role of leaders regarding providing advice/training to staff re maximising hybrid/flexible working arrangements, and setting limits	Change institutional narrative around value proposition (teaching outputs akin to research outputs) Include wellbeing as a standing item on meeting agendas Ensure access to journey-sharing opportunities (such as attending- and/or presenting work outcomes to- conferences, making space for collaborations, undertaking shared scholarship or teaching projects etc) Explore opportunities for partnering between academic and professional staff Leaders actively role-modelling a healthy work-life balance, setting limits, turning off	Personal growth Environmental mastery
Adapt workload models to account for changing role requirements Act on opportunities to move repetitive or administrative tasks to digital systems Design /provide mentoring programmes that meet the needs of modern academics	Providing opportunities for staff with different skill sets to partner together (focus on strengths, rather than "doing it all") Become a mentor and/or a mentee Use wellbeing as a lens through which weighting of tasks, and determination of "appropriate" time allocations and funding are identified	Self-acceptance Positive relationships

(Continued)

Table 6.1 (Continued)

Formal action	Informal action	In support of (Ryff factors)
Provide opportunities for academics, at all stages of their career to, to have their voices heard	Too much autonomy can be an issue in higher education (silos, isolation): informal measures to address isolation can include a simple coffee catch up, or reaching out when a colleague's strength or knowledge might benefit a task you would otherwise just internalise	Autonomy
Ensure policies and institutional procedures (e.g., promotions frameworks) support career progression via differing skillsets Formal recognition (in policy and via mainstreaming of narratives) of the role academic wellbeing plays in achieving institutional goals	Allow for job-crafting (e.g., teaching focus or research focus etc) so academics can focus on their passions and strengths Normalising taking time to improve personal wellbeing outcomes	Purpose in life

formal and informal actions that can be taken by institutions and individuals, to support wellbeing in academia, and ultimately ensure the health and success of its most important asset: Its people.

We live in a world of constant change – the pace of which seems to ever increase – and yet our university systems and processes are largely mired in traditional and out-dated assumptions and practices. It is clear that the time has come for this dichotomy to be examined. There needs to be a realignment of institutional cultural norms to meet the current and future needs of university staff.

Reflections from Chapter Authors

The authors of this chapter came together as a team during one of the many university restructures that COVID-19 imposed on the Australian higher education sector. A silver lining of these changes was the sense of camaraderie that we felt as we embarked on shared endeavours such as writing this chapter. This experience provided us with the chance for both individual and collective introspection, delving into the significance of our work and its impact within the larger tapestry of human existence (see Figure 6.2).

Figure 6.2 Rethinking What You Do and How You Do It
Source: Co-created with Adobe Photoshop

Our collective takeaways from this experience are as follows:

- A realisation of the profound significance of self-fulfilment in our respective pursuits. However, the paths leading to this state of self-acceptance and what truly defines fulfilment remain remarkably divergent, unveiling an intricate constellation of individual journeys united within a shared undertaking.
- The pandemic's unwelcome intrusion broke down many of the silos we had previously accepted (between work and life, between disciplines within the university, between academic and professional staff) due to the magnitude of our common experience. And thus, a lesson emerged: These partitions, these fences, need not be rebuilt, for they offer no enduring purpose.
- Empowered by these realisations, we appreciate our agency in shaping our well-being in the workplace far more than we had initially realised. To actualise this, it is important that we each understand what makes work meaningful for us individually, and to have institutional leadership and an organisational culture that supports personal growth and passions.

References

Bell, A. S., Rajendran, D., & Theiler, S. (2012). Job stress, wellbeing, work-life balance and work-life conflict among Australian academics. *E-Journal of Applied Psychology, 8*(1), 25–37.

Blackmore, J. (2020). The carelessness of entrepreneurial universities in A world risk society: A feminist reflection on the impact of Covid-19 in Australia. *Higher Education Research and Development, 39*(7), 1332–1336.

Branand, B., & Nakamura, J. (2017). The Well-Being of Teachers and Professors. *The Wiley Blackwell Handbook of the Psychology of Positivity and Strengths-Based Approaches at Work,* 466.

Channing, J. (2022). Calculating the pace of change during the COVID-19 era. *The Department Chair, 33,* 4–5.

Christiansen, B. (2022). University business education for the "New global normal". In A. K. Zhuplev, Robert (Ed.), *Global trends, dynamics, and imperatives for strategic development in business education in an age of disruption.* IGI Global.

Rosemary, M., Ekechukwu, O., & Horsfall, M. N. (2015). Academic mentoring in higher education: A strategy to quality assurance in teacher education in Nigeria. *European Journal of Research and Reflection in Educational Sciences, 3*(2), 37–45.

Fetherston, C., Fetherston, A., Batt, S., Sully, M., & Wei, R. (2021). Wellbeing and work-life merge in Australian and UK academics. *Studies in Higher Education, 46*(12), 2774–2788.

Freeman, S. Jr, & Kochan, F. (2019). Exploring mentoring across gender, race, and generation in higher education: An ethnographic study. *International Journal of Mentoring and Coaching in Education, 8*(1), 2–18.

Gewin, V. (2021). Pandemic burnout is rampant in academia. *Nature, 591*(7850), 489–491.

Glass, C. R., Bista, K., & Lin, X. (Eds.). (2021). *The experiences of international faculty in institutions of higher education: Enhancing recruitment, retention, and integration of international talent.* Routledge.

Goerisch, D., Basiliere, J., Rosener, A., McKee, K., Hunt, J., & Parker, T. (2019). Mentoring with: Reimagining mentoring across the university. *Gender, Place and Culture, 26*(12), 1740–1758.

Guppy, N., Verpoorten, D., Boud, D., Lin, L., Tai, J., & Bartolic, S. (2022). The post-COVID-19 future of digital learning in higher education: Views from educators, students, and other professionals in six countries. *British Journal of Educational Technology, 53*(6), 1750–1765.

Hobson, A. J., & van Nieuwerburgh, C. J. (2022). Extending the research agenda on (ethical) coaching and mentoring in education: Embracing mutuality and prioritising well-being. *International Journal of Mentoring and Coaching in Education, 11*(1), 1–13.

Huang, X. (2019). Understanding Bourdieu-cultural capital and habitus. *Review of European Studies, 11(3),* 45–49.

Jia, K., Zhu, T., Zhang, W., Rasool, S. F., Asghar, A., & Chin, T. (2022). The linkage between ethical leadership, well-being, work engagement, and innovative work behavior: The empirical evidence from The higher education sector of China. *International Journal of Environmental Research and Public Health, 19*(9), 5414.

Jones, G. A., & Weinrib, J. (2022). The changing context of academic work: Fragmentation, institutional horizontal diversity and vertical stratification. In *Research handbook on academic careers and managing academics* (pp. 36–46). Edward Elgar Publishing.

Kligyte, G. (2021). The logics of collegial practices: Australian And new Zealand/Aotearoa perspectives. *Higher Education, 81,* 843–864.

Lema, T., & Joullié, J.-E. (2015). Casualization of academics in the Australian higher education: Is teaching quality at risk? *Research in Higher Education Journal, 28,* 1–11.

Littleton, E., & Stanford, J. (2021). An avoidable catastrophe: Pandemic job losses in higher education and their consequences. Centre for Future Work. Retrieved from https://apo.org.au/node/314011

Machin, T. (2020). Enhancing wellbeing for academics. *InPsych*, *42*(1), 1–4. Retrieved from https://psychology.org.au/for-members/publications/inpsych/2020/february-march-issue-1/enhancing-wellbeing-for-academics

Marchant, T., & Wallace, M. (2013). Sixteen years of change for Australian female academics: Progress or segmentation? *Australian Universities. Review*, *55*(2), 60–71.

Miner, K. N., January, S. C., Dray, K. K., & Carter-Sowell, A. R. (2019). Is it always this cold? Chilly interpersonal climates as a barrier to the well-being of early-career women faculty in STEM. *Equality, Diversity and Inclusion: An International Journal*, *38*(2), 226–245.

Mitchell, L. D. (2018). What makes an effective mentor: A cross-cultural (BRIC) comparison. In P. Kumar (Ed.), *Exploring dynamic mentoring models in India*: Palgrave Macmillan.

Mudrak, J., Zabrodska, K., Kveton, P., Jelinek, M., Blatny, M., Solcova, I., & Machovcova, K. (2018). Occupational well-being among university faculty: A job demands-resources model. *Research in Higher Education*, *59*, 325–348.

Nuel, O. I. E., Peace, N. N., & Ifechi, A. N. (2021). Mentoring: The way to academic excellence. *Education Quarterly Reviews*, *4*(1), 130–140.

Osam, K., Shuck, B., & Immekus, J. (2020). Happiness and healthiness: A replication study. *Human Resource Development Quarterly*, *31*(1), 75–89.

Riordan, S. (2011). Paths to success in senior management. In B. W. Bagilhole (Ed.), *Gender, power and management: A cross-cultural analysis of higher education* (pp. 110–139). Palgrave Macmillan.

Ryff, C. D. (2014). Psychological well-being revisited: Advances in the science and practice of eudaimonia. *Psychotherapy and Psychosomatics*, *83*, 10–28.

Ryff, C. D., & Keyes, C. L. M. (1995). The structure of psychological well-being revisited. *Journal of Personality and Social Psychology*, *69*(4), 720.

Schimanski, L. A., & Alperin, J. (2018). The evaluation of scholarship in academic promotion and tenure processes: Past, present, and future. *F1000 Research*, *7*, 1–20.

Seipel, M. T., & Larson, L. M. (2018). Supporting non-tenure-track faculty well-being. *Journal of Career Assessment*, *26*(1), 154–171.

Sorensen, G., Dennerlein, J. T., Peters, S. E., Sabbath, E. L., Kelly, E. L., & Wagner, G. R. (2021). The future of research on work, safety, health and wellbeing: A guiding conceptual framework. *Social Science & Medicine*, *269*, 113593.

Stavraki, M., García Márquez, R., Bajo Romero, M., Callejas Albiñana, A. I., Paredes Sansinenea, B., & Díaz Méndez, D. N. (2022). Brief version of the Ryff Psychological Well-Being Scales for children and adolescents: evidence of validity. *Psicothema*.

Taberner, A. M. (2018). The marketisation of the English higher education sector and its impact on academic staff and the nature of their work. *International Journal of Organizational Analysis*, *26*(1), 129–152.

Trevisan, O., De Rossi, M., & Grion, V. (2020). The positive in the tragic: Covid pandemic as an impetus for change in teaching and assessment in higher education. *Research on Education and Media*, *12*(1), 69–76.

Urbina-Garcia, A. (2020). What do we know about university academics' mental health? A systematic literature review. *Stress and Health*, *36*(5), 563–585.

Van Dierendonck, D., & Lam, H. (2023). Interventions to enhance eudaemonic psychological well-being: A meta-analytic review with Ryff's scales of psychological well-being. *Applied Psychology: Health and Well-Being*, *15*(2), 594–610.

Vesty, G., Sridharan, V. G., Northcott, D., & Dellaportas, S. (2018). Burnout among university accounting educators in Australia and New Zealand: Determinants and implications. *Accounting & Finance*, *58*(1), 255–277.

Welch, A. (2022). COVID crisis, culture wars and Australian higher education. *Higher Education Policy, 35*, 673–691.

Wisker, G., & Robinson, G. (2016). Supervisor wellbeing and identity: Challenges and strategies. *International Journal for Researcher Development, 7*(2), 123–140.

Wray, S., & Kinman, G. (2022). The psychosocial hazards of academic work: An Analysis of trends. *Studies in Higher Education, 47*(4), 771–782.

Zawacki-Richter, O., Marín, V. I., Bond, M., & Gouverneur, F. (2019). Systematic review of research on artificial intelligence applications in higher education–where are the educators? *International Journal of Educational Technology in Higher Education, 16*(1), 1–27.

Conclusion

Lessons Learnt

Angela R. Dobele and Lisa Farrell

Conclusion

We intended this book to aid discussions, provide innovative and meaningful examples to enhance workplace wellbeing, and the skills to create further innovations to push the boundaries of best practice forward. By showcasing real-life wellbeing approaches, we sought to distil meaning and purpose around who we are and how we cope.

As part of our reflections on the creation of this book, we created a word cloud from the reflection narratives of each of our authors' chapters, including our own, see Figure C.1. Three things were immediately obvious. First, what really stands out is workplace culture, there is a very definite awareness that wellbeing is a function of workplace culture (for example in the phrases *staff organisational workplace*, *central systems* and *policies* are most prominently displayed on the top left hand side of our word cloud). Second, the image reflects the importance of wellbeing through social connections (for example, *colleagues, support, shared, experience* and *together*), most predominately represented in the top right section of the word cloud. Our takeaway, from the first and second themes, was the recognition that achieving workplace wellbeing is not restricted to a solo endeavour, wellbeing cannot be an exclusively individual pursuit. The third highlight was the evidence of tensions between wellbeing and career success as a clear theme, in the myriad forms that such success can be experienced and represented (for example, in the terminology around *guidance, feedback, understand, journey, career* and *storytelling*) and most predominantly represented in the bottom of the word cloud. Through this theme we gained a deeper perspective around wellbeing versus career (development or progression) and realised an alternative perspective may be called for, one that considers everyday wellbeing as more than an exclusively personal endeavour, but as part of a much broader conversation.

These themes, workplace culture, social connection and wellbeing woven throughout career, highlight the complexity in terms of the different groups that matter in achieving academic wellbeing. The joint responsibility (individual and employee), connected responsibility (individual and colleagues) and personal responsibility (individual and their career). When reflecting on these themes we both

DOI: 10.4324/9781003284772-10

Figure C.1 Word Cloud From the Author's Reflection Statements.

realised that too often we had held only ourselves responsible for delivering on our wellbeing goals to the detriment of our wellbeing. Recognition that it takes a workplace of like-minded professionals to achieve a culture of wellbeing is a release from the persistent pressure of personal responsibility. Moreover this insight is powerful in motivating action to follow the guidance, advise, and pathways to wellbeing suggested by our chapter authors. Only through a collective movement that academia can take the necessary steps to being a psychologically healthy workplace.

The higher education industry and individual institutions have experienced much disruption in the last twenty years, including increased competition, changing cost and funding variables, role of politics and government, COVID-19, the types of programs they offer and the methods of distribution, digital and technological offerings, changes in student cohorts and characteristics, accessibility and inclusion, financing, services offered, sustainability and, of course, last but not least, wellbeing concerns. It is important to ensure that wellbeing is a key component of decision-making and thought processes and that it receives positive attention without fear, blame or stigma attached. Given the massive disruptions we have just lived through and the increasingly competitive and stressful landscape of the higher education industry, now is the time for a revised model of the future. Overarching, as reflected in our word cloud, these new goals must be centred at the heart of wellbeing.

Series Appendix

Wellbeing and Self-care in Higher Education
Editor: Narelle Lemon

Healthy Relationships in Higher Education
Promoting Wellbeing Across Academia
Edited by Narelle Lemon
In this edited collection, authors navigate how they view relationships as a crucial part of their wellbeing and acts of self-care, exploring the "I", "We", and "Us" at the centre of self-care and wellbeing embodiment.

Creating a Place for Self-care and Wellbeing in Higher Education
Finding Meaning Across Academia
Edited by Narelle Lemon
In this edited collection, the authors navigate how they find meaning in their work in academia by sharing their own approaches to self-care and wellbeing.

Creative Expression and Wellbeing in Higher Education
Making and Movement as Mindful Moments of Self-care
Edited by Narelle Lemon
This book focuses on the lived experiences of higher education professionals working in the face of stress, pressure and the threat of burnout and how acts of self-care and wellbeing can support, develop and maintain a sense of self.

Reflections on Valuing Wellbeing in Higher Education
Reforming our Acts of Self-care
Edited by Narelle Lemon
Designed to support readers working in higher education, this volume focuses on individual and collective practices of creativity, embodiment and movement as acts of self-care and wellbeing highlighting how connection to hand, body, voice and mind can be essential to this process.

Practising Compassion in Higher Education
Caring for Self and Others Through Challenging Times
Edited by Narelle Lemon, Heidi Harju-Luukkainen and Susanne Garvis
Presenting a collective international story, this book demonstrates the importance of compassion as an act of self-care in the face of change and disruption, providing guidance on how to cope under trying conditions in higher education settings.

Women Practicing Resilience, Self-care and Wellbeing in Academia
International Stories from Lived Experience
Edited by Ida Fatimawati Adi Badiozaman, Voon Mung Ling and Kiran Sandhu
Through a lens of self-care and wellbeing, this book shares stories of struggle and success from a diverse range of women in academia, illustrating the ways that higher education institutions can be more accommodating of the needs of women.

Writing Well and Being Well for Your PhD and Beyond
How to Cultivate a Strong and Sustainable Writing Practice for Life
Katherine Firth
Prioritising wellbeing alongside academic development, this book provides practical advice to help students write well, and be well, during their PhD and throughout their career. Relevant at any stage of the writing process, this book will help doctoral students and early career researchers to produce great words that people want to read, examiners want to pass and editors want to publish.

Prioritising Wellbeing and Self-Care in Higher Education
How We Can Do Things Differently to Disrupt Silence
Edited by Narelle Lemon
This book illuminates international voices of those who feel empowered to do things differently in higher education, providing inspiration to those who are seeking guidance, reassurance, or a beacon of hope.

Navigating Tensions and Transitions in Higher Education
Effective Skills for Maintaining Wellbeing and Self-care
Edited by Kay Hammond and Narelle Lemon
With a focus on skills development, this book provides guidance on how to navigate transitions between career stages in higher education and how to maintain wellbeing in the process. Written with all career stages in mind, this book will be an essential resource for new and experienced researchers alike.

Sustaining Your Wellbeing in Higher Education
Values-based Self-Care for Work and Life
Jordan Cummings
This book provides an evidence-based approach to sustainable self-care, anchoring these strategies in individual academics' core personal values. It teaches readers how to use their values to leverage self-care strategies into a workable, individualised, and effective map to wellness.

Passion and Purpose in the Humanities
Exploring the Worlds of Early Career Researchers
Edited by Marcus Bussey, Camila Mozzini-Alister, Bingxin Wang
and Samantha Willcocks
In the spirit of guiding emerging researchers in higher education, this book features twenty unique essays by emergent scholars who weave their personal lives into their research passions, offering a window into the experience of researchers in both professional and personal developments.

Exploring Time as a Resource for Wellness in Higher Education
Identity, Self-care and Wellbeing at Work
Edited by Sharon McDonough and Narelle Lemon
Bringing together international perspectives, this book demonstrates the importance of reframing time in higher education and how we can view it as a resource to support wellbeing and self-care. Whether it's making time, having time, or investing in time, this book explores strategies and reflections necessary to grow, maintain, and protect wellbeing.

Supporting and Promoting Wellbeing in the Higher Education Sector
Practices in Action
Edited by Angela R. Dobele and Lisa Farrell
This book examines academic wellbeing from both institutional and individual perspectives, highlighting innovative approaches to support and promote the psychological health of faculty in an increasingly volatile higher education landscape. Featuring evidence-based practices and firsthand accounts, the book equips readers with practical ideas and strategies they can implement to become wellbeing champions within their own workplaces.

Understanding Wellbeing in Higher Education of the Global South
Contextually Sensitive and Culturally Responsive Perspectives
Edited by Youmen Chaaban, Abdellatif Sellami and
Igor Jacky Dimitri Michaleczek
This volume presents an alternative conceptualisation of wellbeing in higher education, grounded in the socio-cultural context of the Global South. By delineating a contextually sensitive and culturally responsive perspective, the edited book challenges dominant Western notions of wellbeing and invites readers to explore the complexity and multi-dimensionality of this construct across diverse educational settings.

For more information about this series, please visit: www.routledge.com/Wellbeing-and-Self-care-in-Higher-Education/book-series/WSCHE

For Product Safety Concerns and Information please contact our EU
representative GPSR@taylorandfrancis.com
Taylor & Francis Verlag GmbH, Kaufingerstraße 24, 80331 München, Germany

www.ingramcontent.com/pod-product-compliance
Lightning Source LLC
Chambersburg PA
CBHW052013270326
41929CB00015B/2897